AF540248

Malignant Growth

Amit Bhaduri

MALIGNANT GROWTH

Amit Bhaduri

First Published 2016

ISBN 978-93-5002-395-2 (HB)

Published by

AAKAR BOOKS

28 E Pocket IV, Mayur Vihar Phase I, Delhi 110 091

Phones : 011 2279 5505, 2279 5641

aakarbooks@gmail.com; www.aakarbooks.com

Designed by

Limited Colors, Delhi 110 092

Printed at

Sapra Brothers, Delhi 110 092

Contents

Acknowledgement

These essays written for various occasions, appeared first in different places, often under different titles over a period of time. Only the piece ‘There is a little bit of SAIL in everybody’s life’ was first published in *Filhaal* in Hindi in March 2015 and has not been published before in English.

The opening essay ‘Malignant Growth: The Solution is the Problem’ was originally published online by Roza Luxemburg Foundation, Berlin.

`The Ceaseless Hunt’ was originally given as Pradhan H Prasad Memorial Lecture 2009 at Patna, organized by *Filhaal* and a revised version was subsequently published with the title `Recognise this Face’ in *Economic and Political Weekly*, Nov 20, 2010 and in Hindi in *Filhaal*, January 2011.

‘When Democracy Devours its own Children’ was originally published as two separate essays in *Outlook* and *Frontier* and a revised version with a different title in Hindi in *Filhaal.*

An earlier version of `Development by Dispossession’ was published in *Economic Yarlasim*, Gazi University, Turkey, and Hindi in *Filhaal*, December 2014, and a formal model for the arguments in this essay was subsequently formulated and is included here as the sixth essay.

‘Climate Change of Another Kind’ is a thoroughly revised and extended version of a paper written originally for a conference in Poland to honour the memory of Michael Kalecki and published in *The Economic and Labour Relations Review*, 23(3), Australia at the request of Geoffrey Harcourt and subsequently published in *Economic and Political Weekly*, May 11, 2013, and in Hindi in *Filhaal*, August 2014.

'What Remains of the Theory of Demand Management in a Globalizing World' was originally published in Public Policy Brief Series by Levy Economics Institute of Bard College, New York and published in Hindi in *Filhaal*, November 2014.

'Effective Demand under Financialization: An Analytical Introduction' was written for a lecture before a gathering of European Trade Unions and was published on line by the Labour Chamber of Commerce, Austria, and in Hindi in *Filhaal* in May 2015.

'Nationalism and Economic Development' was given as t foundation day lectures at AN Sinha Institute of Social Studies, Patna; Centre for Multidisciplinary Research, Dharwar; and VKRV Rao Institute for Economic and Social Change, Bangalore in 2015 and published in Hindi in *Filhaal*, November 2015.

'On Inequality, Economic Power and Democracy' was originally written for the lecture on the occasion of the award of Leontief Prize 2016 for `Advancing the Frontiers of Economic Thought' by the Global Development and Environment Institute at the Tufts University, USA and a revised version published with the title `On Democracy, Corporations and Inequality' in *Economic and Political Weekly*, March 23, 2016 and in Hindi by *Filhaal,* April 2016.

A collection of Hindi translations of all these essays except the last two have been published with the title *Anachari Vikas* by Filhaal Trust in 2015.

Introduction

This book brings together a selection of essays by Amit Bhaduri, a foremost economist of our time who has just been awarded the Leontief Prize 2016 for 'advancing the frontiers of economic thought' and 'to celebrate his continuing efforts to expand our knowledge of economic systems in the context of globalization, capital accumulation and the shifting balance of power away from governments to the markets'. He is an economist whose works even the Supreme Court of India has taken recourse to. While characterizing the ongoing process of economic development in India as the 'amoral political economy that the State endorses' the Court could not resist quoting at length from his essay 'Development or Developmental Terrorism' in its July 5, 2011 Order (page 6, para 5) in writ petition (civil) No 250 of 2007.

These essays written over the last five years, subsequent to his collection of essays *The Face You Were Afraid to See* (Penguin: 2009) and *Essays in the Reconstruction of Political Economy* (Aakar: 2010) might appear disparate written as they were at different points of time and for different audiences, but they take forward the argument of his earlier collections that the ideology of high growth which has been adopted as the dogma by successive governments at the centre and states is excluding the poor, disenfranchising them from the growth process and destroying their livelihood without creating alternative jobs. Two recent statistics capture the saga of jobless growth in India today. The Labour Bureau's survey in eight labour intensive industries put the job creation in 2015 at a meager

1.35 lakh compared to 4.9 lakh in 2014 and 12.5 lakh in 2009. And the much trumpeted 'Make in India Week' in February 2016 yielded investment commitments of $ 225 billion over five years with a potential job creation of just 6 million!

The author aptly terms this process as malignant growth that is being achieved by dispossession of the poor not only from their traditional sources of livelihood but also from what goes in the name of parliamentary democracy which, as he rightly says has 'shrunk to a level of no choice'. Indian economy might be doing well (although even that is now doubtful and the spokespersons of the grand illusion have to resort to constant redefinition and revision of the base of gross domestic product to show continuing high growth), but the people, almost three fourth of India's population are definitely not doing well as the specter of hunger, malnutrition, growing despair, anger and suicides, not only of housewives, farmers and workers but increasingly of the young stalk the villages and the cities of India. Latest data suggest that suicide has become the leading cause of death among the youngsters.

Nothing is accidental in this process. Everything is deliberate. Keeping the poor in wretched condition and dispossessing them from their livelihood in the natural sector is deliberate so that the ranks of footloose labour on the outskirts of the world class and soon to be 'smart cities' of India continue to swell to provide the rich with a variety of third world luxuries. For the first time in the history of India, five million farmers have been leaving farming every year since 2004–05 as farm income have collapsed and farming has become increasingly unviable.

A 'dangerous mutualism', to use the author's words has come to develop between the private corporate sector and the government by 'infusing the institution of democracy' with the 'ideology of higher growth' as huge concessions are given to the corporate in budget after budget even as public sector banks continue to write off their loans running into hundreds of thousands of cores year after year (the mind blowing figures of nonperforming assets and corporate debt restructuring cases to be of the order of Rs 6 lakh crore in 2015 alone and likely to exceed Rs 10 lakh crore when official numbers are released have just been reported).

The author writes about the 'in-built insensitivity to poverty' that Indian democracy has acquired over a period of time and says that in recent years this has turned into 'arrogant defiance' of the poor in the name of promoting high growth as the 'pretence of assault on poverty' is being turned into 'an assault on the poor, dispossessing them of their land and livelihood, community and culture'.

The author posits this 'evolution' of Indian democracy into the larger picture of evolution of the ceaseless hunt for natural resources that has been the abiding feature of imperialism. He goes on to write about the 'gradual evolution' and 'the mutation' that this imperialist hunt underwent with decolonization and argues that the post-colonial societies with their emphasis on consumerist culture cannot desist from this ancient hunt as it is essential for survival of market capitalism. The hunt has assumed such proportion that Indian democracy does not feel shy of devouring its own children.

As a result, exploitation of the majority and their rejection through various forms of exclusion has remained the essential feature of the 'development' trajectory and so has remained the colonization of the 'minds of a large enough comprador class' in societies like India as seen in the TINA ('there is no alternative') syndrome.

As the exclusion of the poor majority for a minority rich is increasingly assuming the form of narrow jingoistic majoritarianism, the author reminds us about the presence of a streak of this narrowness in Indian nationalism that took shape around the anti-colonial struggle and continued through the course of post-independence nation building in which it was believed that higher economic growth will alleviate all social problems and discrimination against the minority communities over time, much like the present ruling dogma that higher growth by itself irrespective of its nature and content will eliminate poverty and resolve the problem of socio economic and regional tensions.

With the empty shell of democracy getting hollowed out of its content and the march from corporate led growth to corporate led democracy continuing unhindered, the author in the penultimate essay of the book has offered three inter-related propositions around which we need to rethink economic development and decentralized democracy in India.

The author rightly concludes this collection by saying that the need for intellectual work has become more pressing so as to challenge the ideology of malignant higher growth and the institution of shallow democracy with alternatives. And in this endeavour, these essays would definitely be of some help to the readers.

Written in a gripping prose and in a simple jargon free style this is a welcome offering at an opportune time. Two of the essays have a mathematical model but the analysis is simple enough for even common readers unfamiliar with economics to grasp.

March 23, 2016 Chaitanya Krishna

1

Malignant Growth: The Solution is the Problem

A wise crack that found wide currency after the collapse of the Soviet system claims that capitalist market economies are good at creating wealth, less good at distributing it. This conventional piece of wisdom sounds less convincing after the recent financial crisis as unregulated expansion of private finance destroyed billions of dollars in financial wealth, and then needed billions more of tax payer's money to avoid total collapse. The oxygen needed by the collapsing financial system was provided obligingly by the state, but as soon as the patient showed signs of life again, these facts were banished from memory. The replenished wealth of the financial sector, a substantial part of which came from the public through the state soon got mobilized to convert inconvenient facts into convenient lies! The ideology that the state is always the problem, never the solution again started gaining currency through pliable media, academia and other powerful lobbyists at the command of big money. Globalization added more fire power to bamboozle the public. The old American saying, "What is good for General Motors is good for the country" may be revised to suit this age of globalization: what is good for corporations, is good for the world!

Wealth carries with it power, both crude and persuasive, inside and outside the marketplace. Inside the market, money rules as purchasing power and, determines what commodities to produce and, for whom. Money power governs the market by manipulating rules and the rule makers and implementers of law. This is done legally through biased laws, and illegally through subverting and corrupting the process of law. The news served by the media is no exception except that its target is to persuade. Indeed 'paid news' is the commodity manufactured and sold for a price. The media shapes public opinion and reinforces corporate ideology relentlessly by manufacturing and giving news the right 'spin' in favour of big business. Even more importantly, by omission or doctoring of inconvenient major happenings, it presents a view of the world convenient to big money, not to our daily experience. And that is the modern paradox: ordinary citizens feel more informed, while gradually they are being robbed of forming independent judgments based on less biased facts, in effect powerless as the show of representative democracy matures. The power of high finance to set the rules are no longer even in doubt; from the rescue package offered to save banks and financial firms from going bankrupt without nationalizing them, cheating the public under non-transparent financial deals, making financial rating agencies interested parties rather than independent evaluators and without being held accountable by law in all these cases. The triumph of money power over law is no longer a hypothesis of some fringe political theorists, but a glaring fact of life under financial capitalist democracy.

Whenever questioned, legitimacy of democracy driven by big money has pet answers. Compassionate proposals like wealth created by promoting large corporations would trickle down to the poor or, growth led by corporations would be made pro-poor through fiscal (e.g. taxation and budgetary) policies of the state or creating investment climate to attract foreign capital are meant to comfort the poor majority rather than challenge the power of a small but extremely wealthy minority. In the mean time, austerity is needed directed entirely at the poor while corporations become more powerful. Rather than the electorate, the credit rating agencies, often in cosy relations with large corporations as their paid consultants, grade the economic performance of democratically elected governments. They dictate terms and, become regulators rather than being regulated, and set the rules of the game for market economies especially in poorer democracies.

The surrender of authority by governments in developing countries comes in many forms. Apparently still concerned with development, they define 'development' to suit their own interests and those of the corporations. The first step is to pretend that growth, especially growth of corporate wealth and development are the same. And the second is to have a set of politicians in power, who are beholden either directly to domestic corporations or indirectly to international capital because they become the main support base. Indian democracy has been particularly successful in evolving towards corporate democracy under the slogan of 'higher growth at any cost'. The justification offered is familiar: unless the size of the cake is increased (we are reminded by the politicians and the media experts) there would be only poverty to share; and its corollary: the increasing size of the cake would trickle automatically down to the desperately poor unless they happen to die in the mean time from a slow death of malnutrition and ill health.

As 'the largest democracy in the world' Indian case is particularly revealing. In Western Europe, democracy based on universal franchise stabilized in the majority of countries mostly after the Second World War, when per capita income in these countries averaged around 2000 US dollars (at constant 1991 prices). Around the same time India also started on a similar political journey as an independent, democratic country, but at a far lower per capita income of about one-fifth of the European average. Things had to be different in many ways. However, they became rather savagely different over time.

In a country where the majority was afflicted by sub-human poverty, universal franchise should have led to an open assault on poverty as the highest priority. And yet, the inability of Indian democracy to make any serious dent into poverty became glaringly obvious over more than six decades of independence. It became a democracy deformed increasingly by poverty and, growing increasingly immune to it. Things got rapidly worse from around 1992–3 with the ushering in of liberalization and market-oriented reforms. Before liberalization, the stance of the government towards massive poverty used to be somewhat apologetic; post-liberalization the stance is increasingly one of arrogant indifference. Despite the fact that at least two-fifths of the population still lives in sub-human poverty and three-fourths have a meager purchasing power of less than twenty rupees a day, the official developmental agenda focuses on high growth. Ill-conceived and badly implemented relief measures marinated in plenty of high sounding platitudes are thrown at the poor from time to time not as their democratic rights but as mercy from the government.

The consequences of this arrogance are horrifying. Roughly 3 out of 4 Indians (around 920 million) are undernourished, India has the largest share and number of underweight children in the world and, ranks 67 among 84 developing countries on a recently constructed global hunger index (China 9, Sri Lanka 39, Pakistan 52, only Bangladesh 68). Even observers sympathetic to the virtues of a market economy conclude that during the years of liberalization (1993–2005), the rate of reduction in absolute poverty slowed down, while relative poverty and inequality of income increased rapidly reversing the trend of the pre-liberalization period. However, the statistics on poverty has to be counter-posed against the incredible spectacle of the rising number of dollar billionaires and the phenomenal amount of black money held illegally in foreign banks to realize the character of Indian democracy that has taken shape due to liberalization. India is producing billionaires at a rate exceeding that of China, Russia and all rich OECD countries (except the United States). In the last five years (2005–2010) the number of Indian dollar billionaires increased from 8 to over 50 pushing Indian democracy closer to a 'democracy' ruled by a handful of oligarchs.

Crippled by the money power of the billionaires, democratically elected governments of all political colour increasingly want to promote corporate led growth and redefine development for their benefit. The present prime minister (Dr. Manmohan Singh, at the time of writing who was never elected) is remote controlled by the party president as the most ineffective politician available. His real political qualification all along has been that, he would never manage to become a political rival to the party president or her family, but can manage to survive in party politics with her help, aided by explicit support from the IMF and World Bank, and the US administration.

Indian parliamentary politics has shrunk to a land of no choice. The official Left is pathetically similar in many ways. A former CPM chief minister (Buddhadeb Bhattacharya), while dispossessing peasants in Singur and Nandigram was disarmingly candid: "From agriculture to industry, from villages to cities, this is civilization. We Marxists never deny this aim. We too want this to happen". Mr. Chidambaram, the current Home (and former Finance) minister agrees wholeheartedly. He wants to dispossess 60 per cent of Indian population as soon as possible and, push them to cities so that the land can be cleared for big corporations for mining, for real estate under the guise of industrialization.

Nevertheless these politicians are spokespersons of a grand illusion. As this economy gets reformed and our democracy gets deformed, the political failure to deal with poverty (except on paper statistics) through liberalization is presented as our economic success in achieving high growth! The economy does well, not the people! The middle class with its opinions shaped by English language media and, aided by a pliable array of academic 'experts' has become the most enthusiastic buyer of the illusion that the politicians and the media sells. The illusion gives them a sense of comfort mixed with pride in a politically legitimate democracy which has embarked on a trajectory of high growth to catch up soon with the rich industrialized world. It is also their hope that, the poor will disappear somehow, become invisible, or can be made invisible in the glittering cities that would pretend to be world class with shopping malls, neon lights, high rises and highways and streams of expensive new cars (caught in traffic jams to give us a leisurely view of their expensiveness). The poor are banished from view, but are needed in large numbers for providing services, combining third world luxuries for the rich in first class cities. So the law administering authorities have a gold mine to tap: they banish the poor from view, and yet for a bribe let them stay in illegal slums on the periphery to provide the services we need.

The media helps enormously in this narrative of a democracy by banishing from view a ruined country side, where small-scale agriculture has been made unviable by government policies. Average per capita net availability of food grain declined in a running average of every five-year period since market oriented reform started in 1991, from an average per capita net daily availability of 475 grams to 440 grams (cereals plus pulses).In contrast in the period preceding the reform (1972–91) it increased steadily in running average of each five year period, from 434 grams to 480 grams. The explanation lies in the arithmetic of slow growth in food grain production which does not keep up with a declining trend in population growth. It is a badly kept secret of the government in spite of tall claims by concerned ministers. And, by playing with the definition of 'poverty line' the Planning Commission is engaged in the game of hoodwinking the public with figures that show a decline in the per centage below the poverty line. In a country where the spectre of hunger, malnutrition, growing despair and anger stalks, it is a dangerous game to play.

Even direct small producers engaged in agriculture do not gain. Indebted farmers commit suicides in tens of thousands every year; in the last sixteen years farm suicides crossed a quarter million (256 913 persons between 1995 and 2010) with 8 top states (in descending order they are Maharashtra, Madhya Pradesh including Chhattisgarh, Karnataka, Andhra Pradesh, West Bengal, Kerala, Tamil Nadu and Uttar Pradesh) accounting for two thirds of the total number of suicides and together have a mildly increasing trend. Again, the National Crime Related Bureau (NCRB), the concerned government agency tries to gloss over the man made suicide epidemic that is haunting the countryside by claiming that they are caused by idiosyncratic reasons, having little to do with growing agrarian distress. Such claims do not stand scrutiny of either field survey data or carefully constructed suicide mortality rate per ten thousand persons by individual independent researchers. The latter shows a marked increase from 9.7 to 16.2 for males and, from 5.9 to 6.2 for females between 1995 and 2001, and an increase in the ratio comparing the suicide mortality rate of farmers to non- farmers. Against this background of widespread distress in the country, children below 5 die thousands every year from easily preventable water-borne diseases with millions in the remoter countryside deprived of everything needed for human existence, from food, water shelter, sanitation, health care and education. Rapidly growing India aided by a corporate financed media does its best to pretend that this shame can be covered up by the statistics of GDP growth!

However, illusions of grandeur are hard to sustain even among the middle class. The less fortunate among them can only be spectators of luxurious abundance offered by liberalization and globalization. Goods are in plenty, but jobs are in desperately short supply. In a comparison of the pre- with post-liberalization period, their mood echoes a bitter East European joke, "Under socialism the pocket is full, but the shops are empty; under capitalism the pocket is empty, but the shops are full".

Regular employment in organized industries is the first major victim of this corporate-led growth process. Corporations typically cut costs by shedding labour through mechanization to enhance their international competitiveness through reduction of unit cost. This requires labour productivity (output per worker) to rise faster than wage so that labour cost per unit of output declines. India has been experiencing a growth rate of output of some 7–8 per cent, but the growth in organized sector employment has hardly exceeded 1 per cent. This means most of the growth, some 6 per cent, comes not from employment but productivity growth. Despite high productivity growth real wages were mostly stagnant in recent years raising both corporate profits and international cost competitiveness.

According to official statistics, between 1991 and 2004 employment fell in the organized public sector, and stagnated in the organized private sector, and the same picture roughly continues for later years. Productivity growth comes largely from mechanization and longer hours of work. Some specific instances illustrate the impact of mechanization. Edward Luce of *Financial Times* (London) reported that in the Jamshedpur steel plant, Tatas employed 85 thousand workers in 1991 to produce 1 million tons of steel worth 0.8 million US dollars. In 2005, the production rose to 5 million tons, worth about 5 million US dollars, while employment fell to 44 thousand. This works out to an increase in labour productivity by a factor of ten. Similarly, Tata Motors in Pune reduced the number of workers from 35 to 21 thousand but increased the production of vehicles from 129,000 to 311,500 between 1999 and 2004, implying roughly four fold productivity increase. Stephen Roach, chief economist of Morgan Stanley reported similar cases of Bajaj motor cycle factory; labour productivity increased by almost a factor of 6 while the number employed substantially decreased.

Such mechanization is considered desirable because of an obsession with international competitiveness at the cost of the domestic market. It leads the government to follow policies that sacrifice jobs. This obsession is reinforced by policies for improving the 'investment climate' and offering maximum benefits to foreign investors in a 'race to the bottom' with rival developing countries. The package consists of tax breaks, degradation of environment, ruthless labour discipline, Special Economic Zones (SEZ), even dispensing with laws of the land to help foreign companies escape criminal offences like in the case of Bhopal Gas tragedy or the nuclear liability law. When on July 30, 2010 a trusted former employee of the World Bank and currently the deputy chairmen of the Indian Planning Commission (Montek Ahluwalia) wrote an email to one of the highest officials(Michael Foreman) of the Bank for relaxing India's borrowing quota from the Bank, immediately came the reply on the same day in a private correspondence to him: "We are hearing a lot of noise about the Dow Chemical issue… I am not familiar with all the details, but I think we want to avoid developments which put a chilling effect on our investment relationship." The side for which the World Bank plays in the name of development is hardly surprising while the government beholden to the Bank continue unashamed to celebrate its subservience to foreign investors as the way to economic efficiency and growth.

The challenge of creating sufficient jobs as a most important route to greater equality and social mobility is overlooked in the name of efficiency, but this benign neglect helps most the corporations; economic advantages accumulate for them at the cost of small domestic producers. With little expansion in regular jobs opportunities, most of the poor join the informal sector. The majority is self-employed who eke out an existence with the entire family including minor children forming a single labour unit. Together the family shares long hours of work at abysmally low hourly earning per person. Their self-exploitation for survival through long hours of virtually unpaid work raises both corporate competitiveness and profits through various sub-contracting arrangements.

The changed ideology of the state under this redefined paradigm of 'development' which promotes corporations in the name of promoting the interests of people fits in perfectly with the Bank's ideology. And of course the misery of the poor deepens. Both federal and state governments in India have converged on the view that pro-poor welfare measures are by and large counter-productive. Consequently, instead of attempting to moderate the adverse impact of the labour market on the poor by providing them with extensive safety nets, the government takes the policy stance that it is fiscally imprudent and inefficient. Privatization of education, health, and many essential public utilities make the poor even more vulnerable pushing them deeper into the debt. Mostly self employed small and marginal farmers meet their rising working capital cost of corporate sponsored agricultural technology or irrigation cost by borrowing from private money lenders and corporate agents selling genetically modified seeds and pesticides. More than two hundred and fifty thousand indebted farmers committed suicide in the last decade and a half, while the government continues to celebrate its efficiency through success in privatizing agricultural credit and sponsoring corporate controlled agricultural technology. The next victim on the line is small, self-employed traders and hawkers through corporatization of retail trade in which Walmart as a major player had on their board of directors the American secretary of state, Hillary Clinton to promote their business in India.

A hidden aspect of the agenda in the fiscal austerity stance of the government is seldom revealed. Increasing openness of the Indian economy to international finance has had a paralyzing effect on many pro-poor public policies. Despite the fact that India imports more than it exports (unlike China), its apparently comfortable foreign reserves position is mostly the result of accumulated portfolio investments and relatively short-term capital inflows from various international private financial institutions. In short these are various forms of borrowed money. The fiscal and the monetary policies of the government need to comply with the interests of the lenders who dominate financial markets to avoid the danger of this capital flying out. They want to create more economic space for themselves through privatization of basic services which goes these days under the polite name of so-called public private partnership in basic utilities. These measures ration the poor out of the market of basic services, hands over to private business typically the profitable part of the business like distribution and management while makes the state responsible for less profitable activities. Corrupt politicians enthusiastically embrace the idea of getting rich overnight by selling cheap public assets for private gain. The austere fiscal stance of the state is justified on the ground that the state institutions fail to deliver efficiently basic services. None among parliamentary parties want to face the political problem of state failure (like graft or massive corruption) politically, but pretends that the market is the solution. As a result the poorest citizens are rationed out by high prices set by private players from markets supplying basic needs like health or education. The Financial Responsibility and Budget Management Act (2003) was a consequence which restricted deficit spending and, cut deeply into welfare spending for public distribution, health and education in the name of fiscal prudence was agreed to by all political parties in the parliament.

These policies aim at not disturbing the 'sentiment' of the financial markets. Since the private banks and financial institutions who park their money in India usually take their lead from the IMF and the World Bank, this bestows exceptional power on these two multilateral agencies to influence the direction of government policies far beyond the money they lend. The market oriented, pro corporate economic philosophy of these institutions comes into play to cause havoc for the poor. Measures sending adverse message to the financial markets like raising fiscal deficit, imposing tax on transaction of securities are out of favour. This hidden agenda is to keep large private players in the financial markets happy.

Over the years Indian democracy has acquired an in-built insensitivity to poverty. In recent years it turned into arrogant defiance in the name of promoting high growth. The rules of the game began changing openly in favour of powerful corporations. The arrogance is being displayed most brutally with violence sponsored by the state to help the corporations to plunder openly of natural resources. The pretence of assault on poverty is being turned into an assault on the poor, dispossessing them of their land and livelihood, community and culture and, if necessary killing those who resist.

Corporations need natural resources for their private profit—water, forests, mountains, mineral resources, coast lines and other traditional common properties. They require access to land. Forcible acquisition of land by the state for the corporations, often under the eminent domain clause or by debauching the Constitution (especially in Fifth Schedule tribal areas) became the core of the development policy. This means not merely nurturing, but precipitating forcibly economic inequality, in the remote mineral rich forest areas, in the country side along river belts. The octopus of development is gradually entangling the poor in its embrace of dispossession and death.

The growth dynamics in operation in India is being fuelled continuously by growing inequality in two different ways. At one end the growth process is driven by a mutually reinforcing mechanism of 'cumulative causation' (a term due to Gunner Myrdal resembling 'strong positive feedback' in engineering) between increasing inequality and higher rate of growth. Each feed on the other to overcome to an extent demand deficiency in the domestic market due to slow growth of regular employment in the organised sector, meagre purchasing power in the unorganized sector and low expenditure by the state on social welfare. Under normal circumstances such a combination would have resulted in slow expansion of domestic purchasing power and market which in turn would have retarded growth. Since India imports more than it exports, in the Indian case this could not be compensated by net expansion of the external market. Such tendency towards demand stagnation due to growing inequality is countered paradoxically by increasing inequality in a selected manner. Since the logic of the market is to produce those goods for which there is enough demand backed by money, greater inequality with rapidly growing income of some top 10 to 15 per cent of the population leads to rapid expansion of a selective range of goods which only the relatively rich can afford. They demand goods that lie outside the reach of rest of the society but the demand for these luxury goods grows even faster than their fast growing income through the operation of the high 'income elasticity of demand' (measuring the per cent growth in the demand for a particular good due to one per cent growth in income at constant prices. As numerous budget studies have shown, 'luxuries' rather than 'necessities' have income elasticities usually well above unity). However, most of these goods cannot be produced by small producers in the unorganized sector or by village artisans. These 'sophisticated' goods usually require far more energy, water and mineral resources per unit value. Thus, while the majority are ruled out from the market as consumers because they do not have adequate purchasing power, they are excluded as small producers because these goods are far too sophisticated, while assault by dispossession of the poor intensifies for meeting the inputs required for producing these goods. Production and distribution are dominated by corporations, and the absurdity of urbanization pretending to create 'world class cities' for the rich deepens the crisis of livelihood and environment.

A semi official report (by Saxena committee) mentioned earlier puts the per centage of poor people in Orissa at 84.5 per cent (Tendulkar report at 57.2 per cent), far above the Indian average. And yet, between 1993–94 and 2004–5 the value of iron ore produced in Orissa at constant prices increased ten times, that of bauxite and chromite more than two times and that of coal more than three times. Of the three most mineral resource rich states in India, 86 per cent of the districts of Jharkhand, 90 per cent in Orissa and 94 per cent in Chhattisgarh figure among the poorest 150 districts in the country.

It has been estimated that, for each industrial worker employed by corporate industrial house Jindal in Chhattttisgarh 124 persons would be deprived even of drinking water. Tatas have been assured of adequate power (320 million watts) and 50 million gallons of water in the Bastar region for their iron and steel factory, while 50 per cent of the people in the region have no assured drinking water and at least one in five has no water for irrigation in surrounding areas. In Dhuruli and Vanshi villages in

Dantewara due to operations of Essar company, 80,000 people will have no source of drinking water (http://www.chhattisgarh.nic.in/govtpolicy/new%20industrial%20english.hmt).

It is not merely a matter of 'rich land and poor people' or 'natural resource curse', but deliberate government policy to lead assault on the existence of the poor in the hunt for natural resources. The richness of land has to be handed over as economic incentive to private corporations breaking the resistance of the poor. And yet, in deference to constitutional propriety this operation must not be called it by its true name of natural resource hunt for the corporations, but operation Green Hunt to fight against the gravest danger to our democracy and constitution.

Many among India's politicians are beneficiaries not victims of this malignant growth. India may be a poor country, but in the last two decades it has produced more dollar billionaires than China, Russia or most OECD countries. Despite overwhelming number of poor, India today has over sixty per cent multi-millionaires parliamentarians to represent the poor! A good part of these millions is made in land and other natural resource deals between governments and various corporations. To secure this process from popular anger, representation through elections in the parliament has been made prohibitively expensive ruling out participation of ordinary citizens. In this process many new billionaires were born (Madhu Koda of Jharkhand, and the Reddy brothers in Karnataka are known examples) and some entered the parliament directly. The composition of Indian parliament is changing to accommodate the rich to 'represent' the poor of India. On a rough reckoning, 315 out of 543 members of the parliament (58 per cent) are crorepatis (multimillionaires); and, among the recent entrants the figure is even higher, 43 out of 54 (i.e. 80 per cent). An increasing number are directly from large business houses representing their particular business interests in parliamentary committees, while a significant minority (about 30 per cent) are in politics by the privilege of heredity. According to a conservative estimate of declared assets of MPs have grown by more than 200 per cent in less than six years. Representation is clearly the most profitable business in town Some available estimates put the price of entry to the electoral process at an average of rupees 80 million per contestant and can go up to 300 million for candidates from major political parties. All major political parties irrespective of their colour uphold our parliamentary democracy by being involved in this game of raising enormous funds mostly through land and natural resource related deals by using state power. Regional governments cheered by the federal state race to the bottom with increasingly favourable terms in natural resource deals, while corporations return the favour to the political class to restrict entry of unwanted ordinary citizens in electoral politics through a high entry price. The name of the game is, for the state to acquire land and access natural resources for corporations in the name of 'public purpose'; its rich natural resources are to be exploited at will by the corporations not necessary for industrialization or urbanization, but even to export as raw materials (e.g. bauxite and iron ore are important) for huge private profits; the state obligingly allows them to retain most of that profit by charging absurdly low royalties and taxes, and without forcing them to rehabilitate those who are being dispossessed and displaced. In return the corporations give huge bribes to many politicians personally and all political parties who are serious contenders in the electoral game to keep them more than willing partners. This has become the biggest source of scam in post- independence Indian history in the name of liberalization (do not regulate corporations), privatization (in the pretext of public purpose, acquire and hand over cheap to private corporations), and globalization (our international competitiveness and prestige need this). The public purpose of the government is to create private corporate wealth through legal and illegal mining, destruction of forests, rivers, coast lines, and fertile multi-crop land, all in the name of development. The media, the intelligentsia and the academia join to cheer India as an emerging global power with roaring growth performance in the well crafted theatre of the world's largest democracy.

However, this is on the surface. It is not simply a matter of private corruption of the political class. The more sinister process at work is to transform irrevocably a representative democratic political system. It is being deformed in a way to leave it capable only of serving a few rich oligarchs. The game of representation is being changed irrevocably by raising the entry fee into politics. Just as the poor are priced out of essential services like health and education by privatization, now citizens in general without party affiliations are being priced out of the expensive race of contesting elections. The political logic of democracy of "one adult one vote' is being brought in line with market logic of 'one rupee one vote' by making the poor voiceless in both respect.

And yet, the show is faltering. Unmistakable signs are appearing of popular despair turning into mass anger. Hopeless despair did not threaten the stability of this democracy. The spectacle of two million children below the age of five dying every year from easily preventable diseases or, one farmer committing suicide every thirty five minutes over the last decade hardly moved the democratically elected governments. Now the government is facing a different kind of problem. Right to land and other natural resources is in the eye of the storm. The state has turned violent against its poorest citizens to internally colonize them for the control natural resources and a demon designed by these policies has been released. With or without democracy, with or without high a rate of economic growth, we will not escape the wrath of that demon. Signs are looming large. Popular movements of all descriptions have emerged in resistance over the vast countryside and in the forests, some violent others non-violent, some organized others spontaneous, some long lasting, others transient.

The resistance movements are at three levels. At the most obvious level, individual peasant proprietors, big and small, fight for their private property right of land; others like tenants, agricultural workers, fishermen, boatmen, cattle grazers, vegetable carrier cart pullers and other artisans, all who depended directly or indirectly on land and agriculture have also a stake in this struggle. At the next level, mostly tribal communities and forest dwellers fight for their survival, their communal rights and a way of life that depends on their forests, their mountains and their rivers. For many of them the struggle for their community and local culture is inseparable from their fight for immediate livelihood because they would not be able to survive even for one generation without them. A middle aged tribal forest dweller in Dandaranya told me that it is impossible for him to survive even for a month in any other way, because nobody in the city would understand his language to give him a job. At a still broader level, it is a fight to challenge a notion of development which only exploits and destroys both nature and the poor who derive a significant part of their livelihood from the natural economy.

It is a popular fight at many levels, by environmentalists against the danger of nuclear energy, the killing of rivers, mountains and forests, joined often by Gandhians with a different vision of development and a vision which often merges with that of the Maoists living with tribals in the forests and learning from them about alternative nature dependent development. Many from the broader urban civil society join as they witness the scourge of corporate growth and the increasing levels of scams and corruption it has brought with it.

A callous government would have no exit, no escape from the volcanic anger of the people. At the moment many struggles, big and small, violent and non-violent, persistent and transient, urban and rural are being waged locally by people on various issues. Many of these struggles are self-organizing to emerge as a larger struggle that is waiting to erupt on a massive scale to engulf us all. Perhaps in keeping with the enormous geographical, historical and cultural diversity of the country and its people, the lava from that eruption would flow in many directions. The fact that nearly one-fourth of the country is virtually independent of central administration, and the government has started a war on its own citizens to recapture those territories with the help of the paramilitary and regular army is an open admission of the shape of things to come.

And yet, the Indian system has an element of absurdity. The formal democratic structure permits, indeed is supposed to encourage dialogue and legal solutions. Indeed, carefully crafted legal solutions are available without stretching the existing Indian constitution. The local community through 'gram sabhas' have the legal power to decide on the use of land in accordance with the 1996 PESA Act in adivasi dominated areas where the problems of resource rich land and poor people are most acute. Using the guidelines applicable to administration areas under the Fifth Schedule of the Constitution, the federal government could help to resolve rather than accentuate any impasse over the land question in those areas. The 73rd Constitution Amendment with the help of Article 243 of the Indian Constitution makes it legally possible to give them sufficient decision making and financial autonomy. Financial autonomy and a different system of accountability without bureaucratic hurdles are the crucial issues in this context. If gram sabhas are made constantly dependent on higher levels of government for funds for every small and local decisions, they are in effect crippled from being effective. A scheme may be explored in which local branches of nationalized bank give funds to the gram sabhas up to a credit limit. If a local body succeeds in using the fund effectively, it gets more funds; if not, it gets less funds in the next round.

However, a pre-condition for this kind of constitutional and legal options is an acceptance of the fact that the corporate led model of high growth is not the solution, it is the problem. It is the problem not only because of growing inequality on which it feeds to create more inequality but even more viciously, the high level of investment particularly in these fields that is essential to sustain this growth process is being incentivized by giving corporate houses natural resources at throw away prices through a deliberate model of accumulation of dispossession of the poor. This accumulation by dispossession, the life blood of India's high growth coupled with an increasingly luxurious life style for the rich is the process that is being simultaneously celebrated by the rich and despised by the poor. It is getting harder to bridge with palliatives of a representative democracy that increasingly represents only the rich in the name of the poor majority.

The compulsion of the situation is a different model of development that releases local people's initiative through participation and genuine decentralization at the lowest level. However, our history like many previous episodes of history is being shaped not by vision, but by the stupidity of those privileged by the system (politicians, bureaucrats and corporations and their middlemen) who see their immediate self interest only up to their nose. Power-holders at higher levels—state or central level political leaders and bureaucracy—refuse to share powers with the lower local bodies. They have a common vested interest in keeping power centralized only in their hand and, hope to get away by creating the illusions of development through large prestige projects while plundering the natural economy and common resources of the poor.

And yet, the model of corporate-led growth that consumed all our economic imagination making us mindless imitators and prisoners of some meaningless growth statistics is fast running out of steam. We are enveloped by a false sense of glory of India as an emerging global power where poverty is a mere inconvenient fact. Those inconvenient but undeniable facts are beginning to intrude rudely the democratic illusion crafted by the media and the academia for the politicians at the service of the corporations. Without imagining an alternative model of development and recognizing the writing on the wall of growing people's resistance to corporate-led growth there will be no escape. There would be no exit for those who fail to see the growing power of what appear to them merely inconvenient facts. The hollowness of a formal and deformed democracy representing only the rich and the corporations would crumble to give way to a more authentic version of democracy for the poor. Stirrings are already in the air.

References and Notes

1. T.E. Weiskopf. 2011. 'Why worry about the inequality in the booming Indian economy', *Economic and Political Weekly*, November 19, Vol. XLVI No. 47, pp. 41–51. It provides one of the most comprehensive summaries available with perceptive comments.
2. A. Krishna and D. Bajpei. 2011. 'Linear spread and radial dissipation: experiencing growth in rural India 1993–2005', *Economic and Political Weekly*, September 17, Vol. XLVI, No. 38, pp. 44–51. An excellent and imaginative study focusing on the spatial dimension of inequality with urban rural divide.
3. On the agricultural sector and farmers' suicide see, P. Sainath, *The Hindu*, Saturday, October 29, 2011 and Thursday, March 22, 2012. (also, http://www.indiatogether.org/opinions/psainath).
4. Srijit Mishra. 2006. 'Suicide mortality rates across states of India, 1975–2001: A Statistical Note', *Economic and Political Weekley*, Vol. 41, No. 16.
5. Regis Debrey. 1996. *Media, Manifestos* (translated by Eric Rauth), Verso, London and New York.
6. Ensensberger, Hans M. 1988. 'The industrialization of the mind' in his *Dreamers of the Absolute: Essays on Politics, Crime and Culture,* Radins, London.
7. R. Bajpai. 2011. *Debating Differences: Group Rights and Liberal Democracy in India*, Oxford University Press, New Delhi.
8. Association for Democratic Rights (ADR), National Election Watch, various issues, press releases, especially issue of September 15, 2011.
9. A. Bhaduri, 2008. 'Predatory Growth', *Economic and Political Weekley*, April 19, Vol. 43, No. 16, pp. 10–14. Reprinted in his, *The Face You Were Afraid to See*, Penguin, India, 2010 (second reprint), pp. 59-82.
10. Pulapre Blalakrishnan (ed). 2011. *Economic Reforms and Growth in India*, Orient BlackSwan, Hyderabad.

2

There is a Little Bit of SAIL in Everybody's Life

On my way to work every day I see this huge bill board advertisement put out by the Steel Authority of India Limited (SAIL): "There is a little bit of SAIL in everybody's life". How true ! The car I am travelling in right now has a body mostly made of steel; the basic structure of the house I live in is supported by of iron bars like the bridge over Yamuna river I cross every day, not to speak of flyovers, malls, railways, ... my everyday life cannot indeed be conceived without steel. In a sense our civilization has not quite grown out of the iron age, I catch myself thinking!

No doubt we are not in that gone-by iron age when people were first learning the use of iron. Now use of steel is considered low grade technology as the knowledge of the processing technology from ore to steel has got improved, simplified and gradually diffused. So you and I usually have to have no special reverence for this as high tech; we feel homely, comfortable and, it is used widely as the foundation of our civilized life.

But then, has it really spread that far? I wonder how much steel is used by the inhabitants living and getting badly polluted near the very ore deposits in areas I have visited where the sky has the glow of being set on fire by the furnace, from Bailadila on the edge of Bastar where the Mittals made their billions due to dubious bounty from the-then government to recent POSCO in Orissa where a Korean company and the government of India and Orissa together are hell-bent on destroying traditional cultivation of pan, beehives along with the breath-takingly green fields and all adivasi areas in Singbhum, Jharkhand where the sign of destruction of land for iron ore is all over? So supposing she could read, how would a forest dwelling Adivasi react to this advertisement? No doubt she would be greatly puzzled, and perhaps somewhat apprehensive because of her experience with iron mining in her area!

Almost certainly iron would be unknown to her as construction material, but she might know its destructive power in more than one way. It is a valuable material which no longer lies underground. She has been forced to understand that. The companies and the police, usually work together, indeed would go to any length to unleash terror to get hold of it. She certainly would not know all this happens in the name of her 'development', for the sake of her passage to civilization and modernization. But she would be forced to become familiar with this developmental terror that dispossesses her community of their land and their livelihood. She might have experienced it directly, or heard about it and lives in constant terror of how this development would visit her land.

The circle cannot be squared with her life experience. The metal road she can walk on and can to reach is not meant actually meant for her to walk along, without running the danger of being questioned as a terrorist or at least a terrorist sympathizer if she lives anywhere near a 'extremist affected area'. It is meant insted for heavy vehicles to transport rapidly the police force and the jawans with their guns and bullets (made perhaps from the same iron ore of her area) to protect her democratic rights to vote for one of the various political beneficiaries of iron mining. The only brick and cement building somewhere in a nearby village is built by the government; her minister as people's representative came to inaugurate although the children who came from all around did not get the sweets they were promised. In a long speech he had said it will provide all kinds of facilities for a dream school for the children and that day, after the function she went back feeling amazingly happy even though they had to go without lunch. That only brick and iron structure meant as a school turned out to be housing the police of various descriptions (CRPF, Border Security), many of them from distant parts of India who do not speak anything resembling her language. Soon she was told she dare not go anywhere near that 'school building'. As a poor tribal person she was a suspect anyway and perhaps an easy game. She may be excused for believing that the 'school' was for terrorizing her. In those regions rich with iron ore she might even have encountered or experienced the superior killing power of iron-made equipment and bullets used by the corporate security forces and the police. Bows and arrows of the tribal men are simply no match. So she like many others of her tribe has to accept the one sided terror of wanton killing, forced dispossession from land forest, river and mountain that she thought belonged to her village. Iron makes it so much easier!

If she could articulate her thoughts (and that too in post modern jargon!), she might have concluded iron is for deconstruction, not for construction of her life! It deconstructs ruthlessly communities, their way of living, their hope and dignity. However, she would not have known that the main architects are "people's representatives". It is her democratic rights through which they have been chosen! Her interests are safeguarded democratically by them through ruthless deconstruction of her life, only to make the way for her being civilized some day. They might be sitting far away in Delhi, Ranchi, Raipur or where ever. Usually the minister concerned for iron, coal or minerals is busy lecturing to a captive audience of bureaucrats and favour-seekers on mining rights on the need for rapid growth and the value of natural resources. This is one subject on which even the prime minister as the minister of coal could not stop and, Mr. Chidambaram in particular had been most enthusiastic. So, instead of talking about tribal woes with development, it might not be a bad idea altogether to deconstruct him a bit (the 'coal scam' involving the prime minister would hopefully will be deconstructed some day, but one cannot at all be sure when the high and mighty are involved in our democracy).

Mr. Chidambaram, having declared the Nehru period of 3.5 per cent growth as the 'lost decades' announced in a Harvard lecture (of course, where else because of his impeccable intellectual respectability; he was educated briefly in Harvard you know?):

> "For well over three decades after independence India adopted a dirigiste model of economic development...That model extracted a price. It also left a legacy that, to this day remains a heavy burden. The socialist jargon has pervaded all walks of life and especially all economic activity...". So enters Mr. P.C. the dragon killer on the scene: "India's mineral resources include coal the fourth largest reserves in the world (reader you would be excused if the unfolding recent coal scam fleets through your mind). Iron ore, Manganese, bauxite, titanium, chromite, diamonds, natural gas, petroleum and limestone." Now listen to him more carefully: "Common sense tells us that we should mine these resources quickly and efficiently. This requires ... a policy environment that will allow market forces to operate." (http://www.mahindra.com/Enewsletter?july-sept07/html/feature.htmal).

He conveniently forgets to mention in his lecture that the state has to use terror to help the operation of the market forces. His Harvard audience with many special invitees for that lecture, captains of industry and big business, naturally excuses his forgetfulness. However, as the home minister of India he saw to it by initiating Operation Green Hunt. And the Adivasis in distant forests soon had to become knowledgeable about how iron can be of used in a variety of ways to demolish them, their society while Mr. P.C. lets loose on them his idea of 'market forces' in support of mining. So the excellent high ways built through the forests of Dantewara, Jharkhand or Sambalpur might not have brought benefits of housing school or hospital any closer to the local communities; 'schools' might have been built might to house Jawans, but the metal roads certainly allowed easier and quicker access of armed vehicles to forest areas as well as transport facilities for iron ore. Soon after the Kalinganagar massacre(2006) in which 13 tribals were killed, a adivasi woman from that area who had lost her livelihood and was breaking stones on the road side for a high way told us how it all happened for resisting the mining interests of big industrial houses (like Tatas, Jindals). In the most matter of fact manner she she told us that the stone she was breaking now was needed to build the road for transporting ore and for resisting its mining her neighbour's son had lost both his legs in that day's massacre. She did not know that after all, 'law and order' is badly needed for market forces to work; property rights however violently acquired have to be protected in the mines. Adivasis in particular have to agree to voluntary dispossession for the operation of unhindered market forces and protection of unambiguous property rights; otherwise state terror is there. They would be seen as posing 'the greatest internal security threat to the county'. It is the Prime Minister's prerogative to distribute coal fields at will to favoured corporations without accountability. Those who lived there for centuries in those areas should know they have no right to land or livelihood. The corporations can then do anything with it, can just hold it and wait to sell it off to make capital gains. And if you happen to have a prime minister who is also the coal minister policies can be made to give away the coal fields to the corporations. In the mean time, adivasis like ordinary citizens have to sacrifice without questioning because the government acts without accountability in the name of promoting corporate-led growth. The land is being handed over the as incentive to private corporations in this model of corporate led growth; occasionally even the public sector companies themselves are doing the job. However, questioning them amounts to questioning the legitimacy of the miracle of high growth that the largest democracy is pursuing relentlessly, no matter how the defenseless poor feel.

The regions for deconstruction of communities, of people for iron can be broadly identified on the map of India: "If India's forests, mineral bearing areas, regions of tribal habitation and watersheds are all mapped together, they will overlay one another on almost the same area" wrote Sunita Narain. Geologically classified, the massive alluvial river basins constitute the prime agricultural terrain, the land for settled cultivation from ancient times. Bordering the alluvial farmlands are the Chotanagpur, Vindhyan and Deccan plateaus that are zones for dry land farming, pasturing and forestry. They are also the repositories of most of the high valued minerals including manganese, bauxite, copper, nickel, chromium ... and of course, iron.

According to a semi-government report (Saxsena Committee) between 1993–94 and 2004–5 the value of iron ore produced in Orissa at constant prices increased ten times, that of bauxite and chromite more than two times and that of coal more than three times. Of the three most mineral resource rich states in India, 86 per cent of the districts of Jharkhand, 90 per cent in Orissa and 94 per cent in Chhattisgarh figure among the poorest 150 districts in the country. Growth of private mining contributes to worsening the poverty of the poor of the area as they are dispossessed of their land, their water bodies and other common property which goes under the control of the corporations with connivance of the state and central governments concerned. Both benefit and no parliamentary political party is altogether left out of this democratic business of doing mutual favour it has been decided by the concerned governments that the adivasis of the mineral rich areas badly need development through deconstruction. In case they try to escape deconstruction, the state can attack on many fronts: rivers, water bodies, forests and mountains and other common resources, indeed anything that help in sustaining their traditional existence. It has been estimated that in Chhattttisgarh, for each industrial worker employed by corporate industrial house Jindal(who was also especially favoured in coal field allocation) 124 persons would be deprived even of drinking water. Tatas have been assured of adequate power (320 million watts) and 50 million gallons of water in the Bastar region for their iron and steel factory, never mind 50 per cent of the people in the region have no steady source of drinking water; at least one in five has no water for irrigation in surrounding areas . In Dhuruli and

Vanshi villages in Dantewara due to operations of Essar company, 80,000 people will have no source of drinking water (http://www.chhattisgarh.nic.in/govtpolicy/new%20industrial%20english.hmt).

The irony of iron is that this war for iron is fought with weapons made from iron by companies and government against the people who originally lived for centuries on the land that held iron in its womb. It is not merely a matter of 'rich land and poor people' or 'natural resource curse', but deliberate government policy of direct assault on the existence of the poor living from the land. From the rich ore deposits of Lohandiguda in Chhattisgarh protected by armed police and company men for the TATAs, to Kalinganagar in Odisha to state owned Bhilai it is the same story of a strange kind of public private partnership against local people. According to reports the government has decided to provide two battalions in the first stage to guard the project of constructing 253 km railway track to transport iron-ore slur from Rowghat iron ore mines (with more than estimated 500 million tons reserves) through Naxal-affected areas. SAIL actually sought 5 battalion (5000 persons) to guard the Rowghat mines spread over 2030 hectares in Kankel and Narayanpur district which feed Bhilai steel plant.

Well, along with the TATAs, Jindals, Essar and the public sector SAIL too has joined.

Indeed there is a little bit of SAIL in everybody's life, even of the adivasis!

3

The Ceaseless Hunt

I

Conflict over our natural surrounding is probably the most ancient of wars. It goes on unabated with its intensity increasing over time as population increases; but more importantly as the orbit of 'modern' civilization expands to blur the distinction between nature and natural resources. It might have started in our pre-history, in some distant and obscure past as fights between immediate neighbours over control of surrounding territories to collect food, to hunt or to access water. It was a complex fight for survival both against human adversaries in hostile environment, and learning at the same time to be a part of it. It was indeed a delicate balance. Nature was still nature, not just a depository of natural resources, and humans like other species had to be both for and against nature in their struggle for survival.

That balance tipped somewhere. The march of 'civilization' came to be defined almost exclusively as a process of domination of nature by man, and his increasing control over all his surroundings, including other human beings. Development of powerful technology made war on both man and nature easier, and civilization came to be driven by the arrogance of growing technological power which made man feel like Caesar, 'I come, I see, I conquer'. Indeed, it was an even headier feeling when the special target was rival human beings because dominating them also meant control of their territories. Slaves became a most valued prize of wars.

All along there have been voices of scepticism against this arrogant display of power in the name of civilization. Among those who thought differently, Spinoza added an almost new dimension to Western philosophy by insisting that the ethics of man is meaningful only as part of the beautiful and harmonious grand design of nature. For the poet Blake, beauty was in the splendour of naturalness. The conventional system of codified knowledge dismissed the intellectual tradition that considered nature animate. It was considered 'metaphysical', incapable of dealing with the natural or physical world. This view had to be rejected because it was incompatible in every way with the ruthless exploitation of nature in the name of human progress.

In 20th century India, M.K. Gandhi became the most original and vocal exponent of this view. In opposing colonialism as an outcome of Western civilization, he articulated a philosophical position in which the principle of non-violence extended beyond human beings to nature. His distrust of machine civilization, of material progress, even of modern science went far beyond modern 'environmentalism'. It was rooted in a system of belief in which nature was animate and, in harmony with man (and God). He propounded his personal, political, moral and economic philosophy from this point of view, which most of his disciples found hard to accept intellectually, let alone follow practically. Indeed the extent of its practicability or even desirability remains uncertain to date.

Gandhi symbolised the culmination of a long intellectual tradition in which the non-violent anti-colonial struggle he led was intertwined with his moral view of the universe. It was both philosophy and politics More interestingly perhaps, it was also a source of inspiration for a few great scientific insights among thinkers influenced by the gathering anti-colonial mood of the time. At the beginning of the 20th century, J.C. Bose (a close friend of Rabindranath Tagore sharing in some ways a similar outlook), became one of the earliest path finders of modern bio-physics demonstrated through laboratory experiments that plants and trees are 'living' and, capable of carrying messages through electrical impulses. The dissenting voices did not die down in the West either. Tolstoy, in particular, shared views similar to those of Gandhi but did not have the historical advantage of combining their moral philosophy with politics in a potent combination.

Nevertheless, the view that nature is animate has remained at best at the margin of our consciousness. The dominant system of 'modern knowledge has on occasions been as unforgiving to this view as the Medieval Church had been to heresy of those opposed to its theology. This is understandable because machine civilization is founded largely on this dominant system of knowledge with a view to conquer nature, not to live in harmony with it. Most recently misgivings have been articulated politically by various shades of the Green movement. They question the consequences of this ruthless 'conquest' of nature as the integral part of civilization and advise some restraint, especially in terms of environmental sustainability. And yet, they seldom pose directly the politically defining question, 'who is civilizing whom for what purpose'?

In a world where the loot and plunder of nature and of people for profit is an inescapable fact, it has always been a politically loaded question. It is most blatant when military force is openly applied; less obvious when it operates through the market mechanism of trade or aid and other forms of diplomacy. However the outcome is similar, particularly in the poorest regions: colonization of nature along with, of those who have been living as a part of it in a largely natural economy.

The problem came into sharper focus as 'imperialism' in the modern context as one nation state began to dominate another despite the oft repeated principle that all nations have equal rights. From the economic point of view, this principle was probably less important in that pre-industrial age when it was less important to engage in the steady exploitation of nature for securing cheap sources of raw materials. Pre-capitalist imperial expansion was usually more inclined towards short-term loot and plunder and political subjugation for greater glory of the invading power. Ritualistic gifts and tributes were exchanged more as symbols of subservience. They were often not particularly useful for the imperial economy. The fact that long distance transport capacity was limited tended to reinforce this pre-disposition of the conquering power.

Things began to change when long distance trade routes on sea made more or less steady supply from distant lands feasible. Portugal and Spain led the way, and other European powers followed. In the process ambitions for the glorification of the empire through territorial expansion began to get inseparably intertwined with economic motive through trade. This indeed was a historical watershed. For more than a century and a half it was the twilight zone of peaceful coexistence between the status of the empire enhanced by the plunder and loot on the one hand, and political domination through establishment of trading and administrative colonies on the other.

However economic compulsions began to upset this balance as industrial capitalism gradually made its way. Factory production conquered local artisan production, harnessed mechanical energy increasingly to augment phenomenally the capacity to produce (Arkwright's watermill and increasingly mechanized cotton spinning leading to textile mills was economic historian's favourite example). Larger steady supply of raw materials was needed to feed factories. At the same time larger production required larger markets for selling industrial products. The world for the first time seemed to be shrinking in terms of its capacity to supply raw materials. Leading masters of political economy reflected the mood of their time. Adam Smith writing in the nascent stage of industrial capitalism hardly mentions limitation of natural resource as a constraint on the wealth of nations. His great successor Ricardo turns the argument around to claim diminishing return on land, a proxy for natural resource, is the binding constraint that would force economic expansion to come to a stand-still stationary state. Marx deeply impressed by the productive power of capitalism and, repelled at the same time by its ruthless exploitation of the workers finds an economic answer to this political question. He assigns to the expanding working class the role of grave diggers of the capitalist system. With industrial capitalism expanding, international economic competition among the then rising industrial powers of Europe led to more intense search for cheaper raw materials in distant lands. At home, wages were restrained in the early phase by the capitalist class against relatively unorganized workers. It resulted in a slow pace of expansion of the domestic market which was unable to absorb the rapidly increasing industrial production of the factory system. Capitalism had to turn outwards not only in search of cheap raw materials but also for markets. One might say, imperialism became the defining face of industrial capitalism at this stage with the double compulsions for access to cheaper raw materials and, to external markets. In this arrangement, the 'metropolis' of capitalism was a group of industrialized capitalist nations who were constantly engaged in implicit trade wars, but which broke into open war among themselves at times over control of foreign territories.

There were many variations within this broad historical pattern in dealing with the dominated territories and colonies. Direct and continuous application of open military force on a large scale over longish period to achieve these ends was usually cumbersome, often far too costly. While brutal and frequent military suppression of the 'natives' whenever necessary always remained a method, a more insidious option was to present a 'human' face of imperialism by coopting a section of the natives. Between these two extremes of direct repression and cooption, the variations that occurred were tinged with prejudices about, race, influence of the climate and, the power of local resistance. They influenced how the colonies were set up and administered.

An analytical metaphor from the theory of games might help at this stage. Use of open force of short duration is like a 'one shot game' in which the two parties expect to encounter only once.

In these circumstances it is a natural economic strategy to extract in one encounter as much as possible—quick plunder and loot, leaving behind a devastated land. However, for steady supply and an external market outlet, the metropolis have to have a strategy of 'repeated' games because the encounter is expected to recur over time. In a violent solution between one shot and repeated game, the territory has to be cleared once for all of native resistance, often by genocide, for the colonizers to settle permanently on the same land. In an apparently less violent solution, the human face of imperialism tends to be more cooperative with both sides coming to terms with their strategic mutual dependence in enlightened self-interest. However, this comforting outcome of game theory requires the parties to have more or less equal power, e.g. access to counter strategies to inflict sufficient damage, so that the nature of strategic interdependence can be driven home over time in repeated encounters. However, this postulate of nearly equal power is hardly the most relevant case for understanding the historical course of imperialism. Instead of voluntary cooperation in enlightened self-interest, the crucial deviation that often occurs is collaboration of the players of unequal power. Sections of the colonized collaborate with the colonizer resulting in various forms of unequal 'patron client' (or principal agent) relationships. However, privilege by its very definition is exclusive, and restricted to a selected few; indeed if extended to include all or most, it ceases to be a privilege (becomes a universal 'right' instead)! Almost invariably imperialism creates and relies on a subset of the colonized population by privileging them as dependent clients in various ways. As its counterpart imperialism also creates the under belly a vast mass of the exploited, oppressed and underprivileged, the real victims of imperialism.

With imperialism poised for its long haul colonial administration has to be compatible with the long-term interests of the colonizers by reshaping the educational and legal structures. The hegemonic culture that gradually gets entrenched through this process becomes for the comprador class the only cultural climate they ever care to know. They breathe as natural air this dominant cultural climate.

Indeed, the victory of imperialism is complete when it conquers not only the land, but colonizes their minds of a large enough comprador class through whom it mostly administers the colonies. Exploitation and rejection through various forms of exclusion of the majority remains its essential feature, because the comprador class as the administering agent of the imperial enjoys privileges reserved for a minority. Indeed, exclusion from the colonial administrative, legal and educational system is the essential structural characteristic of this collaborative patron client relation with rejection of the majority from the system. Economic exploitation of the majority can continue as 'business as usual' because rejection is structurally embedded. Violence by the state lingers in the background except when state authority is challenged.

While imperialism often nurtured a compradore class in the colonies over time, at home it was initially a class project for the imperial power. From its early phase of procuring foreign luxury goods by trade or loot for the aristocracy at home to the later phase when cheap sources of raw materials and external market became a compulsion for factory production, imperialist expansion had predominantly been driven by the interest of the upper classes. It succeeded in transforming itself gradually from being a class to a nationalist project when the economic advantages of imperial exploitation of the colonial periphery began to percolate down to the working class at home. The 'labour aristocracy' at home was enticed to collaborate and became the counterpart of the comprador class in the colonies. Yet another escape route was offered by greater economic opportunity to settle as colonizers in other foreign lands cleared through genocide, extermination or dispossession of the original inhabitants (e.g. North and several countries of South America, Australia).

This transformation of imperialism from a predominantly class to a nationalist project dealt a double blow to international working class movements. The interest of the labour aristocracy became increasingly distinct from that of the working people especially in the colonies, and the labour movements became divided along nationalistic lines. As a result, eruption of imperialist wars among rival capitalist powers got support as 'nationalist' cause from the respective working classes of the warring countries. In relatively peaceful times of milder trade wars, it still continues to express itself through xenophobia.

Territorial domination for access to natural resources got a wider focus as imperialism evolved in three directions. First, colonies were important for providing both raw materials and captive external markets. Second, the doctrine of national security of the home country was useful for dominating adjacent territories, and was presented as the precautionary motive for expansion (Vietnam, and more recently Iraq and potentially Iran are examples). Finally, the doctrine of precautionary security could merge seamlessly with the notion of ideological hegemony (In the bipolar world of cold war it was obvious, now it is regime change for the democratic aspirations of the people).

However gradual evolution of imperialism underwent almost a mutation paradoxically with large scale decolonization. Post colonial societies with their emphasis on a consumerist culture essential for the survival of market capitalism cannot desist from the ancient hunt. Decolonization on the other hand only changed the direction but not the goal of this march. As countries that were once formal or informal colonies gain political impendence, the more successful among them join the march of civilization in the name of 'development' only to become colonizers themselves of even poorer and more defenceless lands. The irony of history only begins, does not end there. The formerly colonized countries are relatively new in the race, and handicapped by an inherited past of economic and military weakness in a world of stronger competitors. And so, the direction and the target of the hunt change. If strength does not allow conquering other lands and people, regions are identified for the hunt of natural resources inside the country. Imperialism in its mutated state turns inward as the late comers in the race wage war against their own citizens in the name of 'developing' them.

By its own logic, the violent hunt follows the international pecking order of power. Among the new entrants to this race, a relatively more powerful country like China has greater ability to externalize its hunt for resources compared to a less powerful country like India (Even then pauperization and proletarization through migration from countryside to cities, some 120 million since 1980, through dismantling of state-owned enterprises, some 70 million and finally, through collapse of rural townships has been massive, possibly unsustainably in China). In this perverted 'nationalist' project, achieving a higher the rate of economic growth becomes synonymous with the speed with which the country climbs up the ladder of power. However, higher growth driven by this logic also means greater pressure for procuring natural resources by dispossessing those fellow citizens who are unfortunate enough to live in areas of abundant natural resources. With effortless ease the old colonial logic of "a white man's burden" returns to haunt the one time colonies. A 'civilized' class consisting of corporate leaders, sleek media persons and the wheeler dealer politicians with a pliant class of bureaucrats, join hands to 'civilize' and 'develop' the uncivilized. Even ethnic details of the old colonial ideology are not left out. The centuries old ancient homeland of the Adivasis (about 8% of the population) in resource rich regions and the Dalits (16%) who are treated as rejects of the Hindu society, together are among the poorest in rural India. Together they constitute just about a quarter of the total population, but account for more than half of those who fell prey to the violently predatory process of high growth. Dispossessed of their land, home, livelihood, family, close-knit communities and common properties, this ethnic war of the 'master race' continues to civilize relentlessly the 'primitives'.

Irrespective of the ideological colour of the political party in power in the states and in the federal centre, all the governments join this hunt with great patriotism to dispossess the poor for making India (or their respective states) an emerging global power. National and multinational corporations are viewed as the muscle powers needed to win the race in countries like India. They are enabled with a special economic steroid by granting them almost free land, water bodies and rivers, mineral resources, forests, mountains, coast lines and anything else they might fancy with the democratic government in India at their service to acquire them for mining, industrialization and special economic zones (SEZ).This becomes the public purpose for private wealth, and corporate wealth grows at a dizzying rate with poverty-stricken India producing billionaires at an alarmingly high rate. They are presented as the face of emergent India which the world is expected to admire.

Irrevocably however the balance of power must shift in this process. Increasingly powerful corporations manipulate with their money power to cripple further an already limping democracy through this gangrenous growth process. Under the empty shell of a multi-party democracy, a new script is written to reverse the balance, and make the principal the agent and the agent the principal. Corporations do not merely stop at bribing politicians, judges and bureaucrats; they begin to dictate terms and their larger compulsion is to transform India into a corporate state. Laws proposed for the special economic zones (SEZ) where corporations would rule supreme read almost like the chronicle of the death of Indian democracy foretold.

However, when history begins to repeat itself it usually turns out to be a farce, at times a cruel farce on those who started it. While development through high growth, like its predecessor imperialism, becomes a class project, attempts continue at giving it the face of a nationalist project. The chorus is joined by politicians, media and the academia to present this as enhancing our 'national prestige' on the international scene while market driven rapid growth becomes the obsession at home. Merciless hunt for natural resource becomes the essential means to this end and, the colonized mind considers this the only way forward in imitation of their one time masters.

The new post colonial comprador class that takes charge of the chorus has an easier task this time. They inherited colonized minds through a bureaucracy that knew law but not justice, a media that considered facts malleable and an academia that had concern for the rulers not the ruled. In recent times collaboration has become even more attractive through offers from domestic and foreign big business, multilateral agencies like the World Bank, IMF and WTO. It is truly a case of successful public private partnership on a global scale to help the privileged compradore class secede from the people they rule. As its natural corollary, democracy maintains its form not its content; it dances on the stage like a ghost of democracy, a shadow without substance in three acts.

Act I: Despite overwhelming number of poor, India today has over sixty per cent multi-millionaires parliamentarians to represent the poor. A good part of their millions is made in land and other natural resource related deals (MOUs) including legal and illegal mining, destruction of forests, rivers, mountains, coast lines, and fertile multi-crop land. The public purpose of the government, is to create private wealth in the name of development.

Act II: Representation through elections in the parliament becomes prohibitively expensive ruling out participation of ordinary citizens. (Some estimates put the price of entry to the electoral process at an average of rupees 8 crores per contestant, which goes up to nearly 30 crores for contestants from bigger parties). Consequently all major parliamentary political parties upholding democracy are in the game of raising enormous funds mostly through land and natural resource related deals. Regional governments cheered by the federal state race to the bottom with increasingly favourable terms offered to corporations in natural resource deals, while corporations return the favour with big money to restrict entry of unwanted ordinary citizens to the charmed circle of the political class.

Act III: In the final act the largest democracy in the world is placed against the background of globalization. The media and academia present a well-crafted image of India as an emerging global power. Occasionally reality intrudes and the script has temporary digression. The play looks unconvincing when thousands die in a gas tragedy and democratic government crawls in front of large international corporations in full view of the audience. However the audience is made to realize that sending wrong signals would vitiate international investment climate essential for high growth. So the play goes on with India as an emergent global power. The script reiterates as its theme song that widening disparities among classes by privatizing basic needs like schooling and health is not a matter of shame, but a matter of pride. Children from privileged classes go to schools with world class facilities, the rich have access to world class health care, and the corporate controlled media focuses on these achievements. After all these are necessary for an emergent global power which would lead the world with the maximum number of undernourished, crippled and illiterate children by the middle of the 21st century. But that is better overlooked as part of the main play.

Our middle class is a part of the cast and, of the audience. It is dazzled by this performance, its own image of glamour. It has yet to realise it might turn out to be a cruel farce ultimately on themselves, a cruel joke of insidious intent which will continue to delude them until overcome by a violent turn of history.

References and Notes

1. Magdoff, H. 1976. *Imperialism: From the Colonial Age to the Present*, Monthly Review Press, New York. Gives a comprehensive short account of imperialism evolving as domination of one nation state by another; develops in particular the notion of precautionary imperialism as formal or informal domination during the Cold War period. This can be complemented by, Michael Beaud, 1983. *A History of Capitalism, 1500-2000*; Original in French (Editions du Seuil) 1981, English translation by Monthly Review Press, New York and Aakar Books, Delhi.
2. On some recent Chinese experiences relating to high growth, see Forester, J.B and R.W. McChesney 2012. 'The global stagnation and

the Chinese economy', *Monthly Review*, February, Vol. 63, No. 9.

3. Amnesty International. 2010. Don't mine us out of existence: Bauxite mining and refinery devastate lives in India, access on www.amnesty.org.
4. D. Roy, 2008. 'Hydropower in Uttarakhand: Is 'development' the real objective?', *Economic and Political Weekly*, October 11.
5. Centre for Science and Environment. 2008. Rich Lands Poor People: Is Sustainable Mining Possible? *State of India's environment: The Sixth Citizens' Report*.
6. M. Kelley and D. D'Souza. 2010. *The World Bank in India*, Orient BlackSwan, Hyderabad. A collection of papers presented at a people's tribunal, many of which are highly informative about specific cases, as well as some general aspects of the operations of the World Bank in India in recent years.

In addition, current information is mostly available online on various relevant websites. See in particular: www.sanhati.com (on special economic zones, also on environment), www.manthan-india.org (on water), www.dakshin.com (on coastlines and port), www.mining zone.org (on mining, especially iron and steel and coal and several others.

4

When Democracy Devours its Own Children

This piece is written to remind the reader that encounter killings are horribly unjustified, far worse than death sentence with insufficient evidence. Fact finding teams from the civil society approved by the Supreme Court should present their findings as to why the killing took place. This would provide at least some check when a democratic state runs amok in the name of democracy!

I

'There has never been a death more foretold' wrote Gabriel Garcia Marquez in his classic little novel *Chronicle of a Death Foretold*.

The setting is a small sea side town somewhere in South America where virtually the whole town knows that an honour killing of a young man is going to take place that morning. The killers wait with open knives in full view of the public declaring to all passers-by their intention. Nothing is kept secret, and the killing takes place in full view of the town through various acts of omission and commission of the public. Everyone concerned has his or her justification why they could not prevent the slaughter. Insights about the gripping power of collective prejudice merge realism with fantasy to create the magic Marquez is known for.

However, even the magic realism of a Marquez falls short of 'facts' reported by Indian law enforcing authorities through the media about 'encounter killings'. These are some of the reported facts about a case.

(a) A man was reported killed but soon returned to give a press interview. Therefore he had to be killed again!

(b) The man foretold more or less exactly the events leading to his own death.

(c) The death was claimed to have occurred in a jungle with magical qualities, where objects defied the law of gravity, the arrow of time moved backwards from future to past.

(d) Finally, the collective prejudice of the powers that be found it fit to celebrate the ritualistic honour killing as the victory of democracy.

Let the 'facts' be deciphered.

II

A Communist Party of India (Maoist) spokes person and Central Committee member, Azad was killed with his wife Rama by the police in an 'encounter' in Eturnagaram forest in the Warangal district of Andhra Pradesh. Soon afterwards a very senior police officer, a former chief of the Research and Analysis Wing (RAW) P K Hormis Tharrakan confirmed the news in an article in a major national daily (Indian Express, 22 April, 2008). However, the news was contradicted within a few days by another man called Azad in an interview which appeared in CPI (Maoist) *News Bulletin* (number 2, 10May, 2008). It explained that Azad who was killed was Gajarla Saraiah, and the Azad giving the interview was Cherukuri Rajkumar, the chief spokesperson of their Party.

Then Cherukuri Rajkumar (Azad) kept foretelling the circumstances of his own death through deaths of other comrades. In a press release of 24 May, 2009 published in all leading national dailies he described how his comrade, Patel Sudhakar Reddy alias Suryam, a member of the central committee of CPI (Maoist), was arrested from Nashik city in Maharashtra by Andhra Pradesh Special Investigation Bureau (APSIB). He " was brutally tortured and murdered on 23rd night... the government floated the story of an encounter killing having taken place in Tadwai forest in Warangal district (where) comrade Suryam and district committee member comrade Venkatayya were said to have been killed. The police claimed that one AK-47 rifle and a 9mm pistol were recovered" In that press release Azad explains how his comrade Sudhakar Reddy was being followed by APSIB since at least a week prior to his arrest. "He was kept under watch when he went to the shelter maintained by comrade Venkatayya in Nashik."

In another press statement (published in *People's March*, May-June, 2010) Azad chronicles how two of his comrades, Sukhamari Appa Rao and Kondal Reddy were murdered on March 10. 2010 in cold blood by APSIB and Grey Hounds, "after being abducted two days earlier from Chennai and Pune respectively, tortured and taken to the Nallamala forests where they were shot dead in an encounter. His press statement asserts that the order to kill came directly from the Central Home Minister Chidambaram. He then wryly observes that, (although) Andhra Pradesh Police and Chidambaram have been claiming all the while that Nallamala forest has been cleared of the Maoists, (they) had not realised that "the so called encounter with such a big Maoist leader in Nallamula region would mock their own claims of the past three years."

And then, a few months later sometime between the night and early morning of 1and 2 July 2010, Azad himself was killed by the same Andhra police. It followed the same encounter script. His dead body with that of a young journalist Hem Chandra Pande was discovered in Adilabad forest. As in the case of Sudhakar Reddy, the police claimed exactly the same weapons, one AK-47 rifle and a 9 mm pistol were recovered beside the two dead bodies.

Like in Nallamala forest where Appa Rao's body was left, the forest of Adilabad where Azad's body was discovered had been reported as quiet and totally free of Maoist activities according to villagers for the last four years.

The discovery of the dead body of a leader of Azad's stature led several villagers to mock the police in private. One villager said to a visiting fact finding team that, Azad had more brains than that of the entire Andhra police force put together, and he would not have been so stupid as to get killed near their village in Adilabad forest.

However, there is a method in the apparent stupidity of the police on which Azad himself had commented earlier. The police throw the dead bodies of Maoist leaders in areas where they were known and admired for their work among the poor people while working over ground. Azad had been a legendary trade union leader among workers in the Singarini coal mines near Adilabad forest.

There has never been the chronicle of a death so frequently foretold so many times by the very person who himself will be killed. And, there has never been stronger collective prejudice manufactured by the media, the political class and big business justifying this honour killing for the sake of 'democracy'.

III

However, there is an omission in all the chronicles of encounter deaths reported by Azad. He never mentioned that peace initiative was meant to kill. The sequence of events that led to Azad's killing are well known. At the instigation of the central Home Minister Chidambaram, Swami Agnivesh, a noted non-violent social worker, approached the Maoists with a letter from Chidambaram stating conditions for a peace dialogue starting with a 72 hour mutual cease fire. On behalf of his party Azad responded positively, but wanted some of the conditions amended like the cease fire to be extended to six months to coordinate with regional committees the cease fire as a prelude to dialogue. Chidambaram then insisted on a definite date for cease fire, Agnivesh suggested three alternative dates, and Azad was traveling widely contacting various regional units to arrive at a date acceptable to them all. In the process, he outed himself from underground. His track became visible to the police, and the rest is history.

With Azad all possibility of peace was killed, and the central Home minister refused to initiate any enquiry claiming it was the prerogative of the Andhra (Congress) government. The home minister of Andhra claimed immediately after the encounter that she had no knowledge at all. Since then both the central and the state governments have maintained a studied silence.

The story of this encounter might have remained buried. Yet the incongruities were too fantastic and began to trickle out through the efforts of a few journalists, human right activists and a handful of members of the civil society.

At 6.30 a.m on 2 July some local journalists got calls from some unidentified police personnel that Azad was killed, two dead bodies (the second body was identified later as that of Hem Pande) were lying in Adilabad jungle. And yet, in a later report written at 9.30 a.m the police claimed both bodies were unidentified. The arrow of time clearly moved backward in police headquarters!

According to police report Azad and Pande were killed in an exchange of fire with a Maoist band traveling from Gorcheroli in Maharastra. The band was at the top of a hillock, and the brave policemen were firing from below. And yet, according to post mortem report the trajectory of the bullet that killed Azad entered his body from above (chest level) and traveled downwards defying the laws of gravity!

The black burnt marks of bullet according to forensic experts also suggested that he had been shot dead at a very close range. Presumably those remarkably brave policemen ran up the hill at a lightning speed and shot him dead at close range!

Azad's death adds a new chapter in discourses on revolutions. We have repeatedly been told in history books that violent revolution devours its own children. However, we have not yet been told how a democratic republic presumably built on the Gandhian foundations of non-violence becomes a deranged killer. In a recent hearing in the Supreme Court Justice Alam orally observed:

Our Republic cannot bear the stain to kill its own children (*The Hindu*, 15 January, 2011).

Can our democracy be saved from such patriotic honour killings of its own children?

IV

Crooked are the times.

Crooked because, peace turns out to be more dangerous than war for those who seek peace.

Crooked because, enforcement of law in the name of peace turns out to be more frightening than the lawlessness of war.

Crooked because, lies are given out as facts by those very politicians who pretended until yesterday that they share the anxiety of the people but possess conveniently crooked memories to do exactly the opposite when in power.

Mamata Banerjee's political fortune began to change for the better as the CPI(M) increasingly displayed an almost pathological arrogance towards the people. Its fate was sealed in Nandigram and Singur and, then in Jangalmahal. She provided the rallying point in parliamentary politics. But below it lay a deeper issue: the anxiety of the poor of being dispossessed of their land and livelihood, their defenselessness against the brutality of state terror used by the party in power. She pretended to sympathise. Many in the civil society thought they had found a leader who was willing to face the issue of arbitrary state power and party terror in which the CPM had indulged. And many had hoped, even if she cannot provide economic relief to the people, she can at least stop the state machinery from brutally oppressing the people.

It took hardly six months for her to dash all such hopes, and exhibit tendencies which rely on police force rather than on the people; on empty populism and utter lies to justify state repression. Killing of the Maoist leader Koteswar Rao (Kisenji), with a fantastic story telling of the encounter given out to the media by the chief minister herself foretells the dangerous extent to which she would go to promote herself against the people with the aid of state terror.

In the Jangal Mahal area of Purulia, Bankura and west Medinipur Banerjee's party had tremendous electoral success, as all but one front ranking CPM leaders were defeated. These were desperately poor areas of west Bengal and sub human poverty had been a part of people's life. The CPM had done virtually nothing to alleviate these conditions during its long years of rule. Poverty had made people cynical about ever being able to change their life through electoral politics. Such cynicism breeds political apathy and despair, possible occasional out bursts, nothing more sustainable.

And yet, what the Jangal Mahal witnessed for quite a while before the election was a growing sense of political restlessness and popular resistance. Anyone visiting the area could feel that something was in the air, perhaps a growing sense of identity of the oppressed adivasis. A sense of solidarity was shaping up against a long history of deprivation, cultural subjugation and most important of all, contempt shown by the state to their life and dignity. Throughout Jangalmahal, the combined central and state police forces and, the CPM supported goons of the 'harmad bahini' behaved like an occupation army in a foreign land with no accountability. They killed, looted and raped. Local resistance initially with leaders like Chatradhar Mahato or Lalmohan Tudu simply wanted their dignity to be restored and an apology from the guilty police officers. The Maoist party provided the backbone of support only from the background, but on all account they were flowing with the popular mood of anger and outrage, but not leading it at that stage. However, the people of Jangalmahal got back in return more abuse and state terror, more arrests and more torture, rape and killing. Fighting the Maoist influence became the umbrella excuse for all kinds of atrocities committed by the police and the party (TMC) to establish its hegemony over the area.

Mamata Banerjee with the experience of Singur and Nandiram had been quick to capitalize politically on the situation by promising

(a) unconditional release of all political prisoners and (b) withdrawal of police forces from the area. As soon as she won the election, she started going back on her promises. Political prisoners were not released and she refused to withdraw the joint police forces until an officially initiated peace process had yielded results to her advantage. And then she played the same old gramophone record played earlier by home minister Chidambaram.

V

Every time the authorities say they want to initiate a peace process they want their armed adversaries to 'abjure violence'. This peace without categorical guarantee of safety from the government is dangerous for underground Maoist leaders who need to initiate first dialogue within the party. In the process they run far greater risk of becoming visible targets for the police who capture and kill them in fake encounters. This happened to at least two Maoist leaders when the peace talk failed in Andhra in 2003, to Azad in 2010, and now it has happened to Kishanji in 2011 with Mamata Banerjee presiding over the killing as the chief minister of west Bengal.

Clearly the state policy all along has been to liquidate illegally its Maoist opponents in the name of peace talk and, Banerjee has not deviated from this policy. She only made herself more ridiculous by telling absurd stories about how for three days the police surrounded and requested him to surrender which no villager (of Sorakata) ever heard. Obviously, she was referring to a silent announcement which only she and her police could hear! Then according to those who saw the dead body, it had unmistakable signs of horrible tortures, burnt marks (under left feet), marks of cutting with a sharp weapon like bayonet (more than 30 marks) and bullet marks. If the chief minister is to be believed, Kishanji must have been shooting at the policemen while his feet were being burnt, his body and face were being cut up by bayonets and pierced by bullets! The post mortem report like Banerjee herself was silent about all this. Finally, the official post mortem report done in Medinipur claimed that the bullets were fired from a distance of at least 500 meters. Although it might fit Mamata Banerjee's fantasy of an encounter, no known rifle used by the Indian CRPF or police is known to have such a long range (between 300 and 450 meters for AK-47 and Insus rifles).

VI

Beyond the land of malicious fantasies and lies, the truth is brutal. Peace talks with the Maoists have become a ploy for trapping and killing them in cold blood. This same pattern has repeated itself over and over again and, the real puzzle is why the Maoists still respond to peace talks. The reason probably is that the Maoists survive mostly on popular support, and, ordinary people everywhere would like to live in peace. It is the pressure of popular demand to which the Maoist leaders yield at great personal risk. Otherwise, it goes without saying there is no trust between the two parties to build the bridge of peace.

For civil societies and concerned citizens vocal in this matter, it is essential to face this fact instead of wallowing in platitudes of the desirability of peace and constitutional rights which the state does not respect, and the Maoists have no reason to respect if the state treat them simply as dangerous outlaws to be killed, not a political party with a diametrically opposite ideology.

There is only one thing we as outsiders can do to call the bluff. Peace talk cannot be initiated in Jangalmahal unless an impartial enquiry is held first into the brutalities and killings committed by the police, and the CRPF and all the prisoners released unconditionally to give evidence in particular cases. Only when the guilty are punished the climate for peace would be created without the outrage of the people being exploited politically either by Mamata Banerjee or the Maoists. But this requires a government which depends genuinely on the people and not on the police. Mamata Banerjee has failed to qualify in the very first round.

VII

Undemocratic 'them' have to be slaughtered by democratic 'us' if they seek peace. They have to be killed if they do not seek peace. They have to be killed and, that is the bottom line. Bottomline of our democracy and also, the bottomline of corporations that wish to control the land, water, forest, mountains, mineral resources of the country. If necessary slaughter them extra-legally, and declare them outlaws because they are the ones who really threaten corporations and therefore, our democracy; kill them in defense of democracy is the imperative of this democracy.

Wars at least do not require pretense to kill. So declare war, but initiate peace process for pretense. And always remember the soothing liberal myth; our democracy upholds freedom. So farmers ruined by debt have the freedom to commit suicide; adivasis dispossessed of livelihood have the freedom to get killed 'accidentally' as collateral damage while the state hunts for Maoists and their sympathisers in jungles; Sharmila Irom too has her very special freedom of wasting away for ten years while the armed forces protect with their special power act, of course only to protect your and my freedom. And we the citizens also have the freedom to watch in silence scam after scam dished out by our democratic government with platitudes in the parliament.

This democracy bestows its less privileged citizens the right to melt away without a whimper of protest, while we have the freedom to listen to pious pronouncements about the sacred rights of elected politicians. We have to abjure violence in war and in peace; only elected politicians have the right to make , break and bend laws to decide whom and how to kill, what is terrorism and practice state terror to protect our freedom defined for us by them with the help of corporations.

Maoists are accused of letting the gun control their politics. What are we to make of a central home minister or, of a state chief minister who lets the gun of their police define our democratic rights?

5

Development by Dispossession

Capitalist development as a transformative process of earlier modes of production has been analysed from different angles through the ages. Adam Smith viewed this as a process of gradual establishment of the market system coordinated by the price mechanism that provides a suitable framework for raising labour productivity through division of labour and specialization. David Ricardo foresaw growing pressure on limited natural resources (land) as an inevitable outcome of this process which would raise the rent on land resulting in distributive conflict between the landlords and capitalists and stifle economic growth. Although Karl Marx is known for placing the distributive conflict between the capitalists and workers at the centre of his political analysis, he diagnosed this transformation as an intertwined historical process of class formation and accumulation. It originates in the violent dispossession of peasants from their land. Dispossessed of their traditional means of livelihoods they are gradually forced to join the nascent industrial working class, while 'primitive accumulation' aided by the legal and repressive power of the state helps the emergence of a powerful capitalist class. Economists in modern times seldom return to analyse the origin of capitalistic development. They tend to celebrate instead the impressive show of capitalism as an ongoing process raising continuously the productive capacity of the economy. Schumpeter in particular captured the imagination by describing it as a process of 'creative destruction' that is driven continuously by innovation and competition to place entrepreneurship at the centre stage. In a similar vein, Arthur Lewis sketched the process of transformation of the dual economic structure of an underdeveloped economy as largely free of class conflicts in which the state takes sides. It is driven instead by the price mechanism, namely the terms of trade between industry and agriculture with unlimited supply of labour at a constant real wage rate in the traditional sector as they gradually get absorbed into the modern industry as wage labour.

While highlighting important aspects of a vastly complex process of transformation, these visions have to be inevitably limited because each narrative is specific to the time and place of the observer. Naturally none fit adequately the specificities of other experiences. Against this background, we propose to analyse in this paper a central aspect of a similar transformation process that has been underway in India in recent years.

As a predominantly agrarian economy with massive poverty, India is attempting to modernise its economic structure through achieving higher economic growth in the specific context in a significantly more globalised world economy and an internal political set up of a functioning multi-party democracy. Achieving a higher rate of economic growth has been identified by successive governments as central to this strategy, particularly since 1991, when market-oriented liberalisation of the economy became more or less the officially accepted doctrine. Sufficient control over natural resources to accelerate the rate of economic growth became an important aspect of this doctrine in which land acquisition by the state from peasants and communities plays the central part.

The term 'development (accumulation) by dispossession' is descriptive of this process, but leaves open the question of the routes by which dispossession is carried out.[1] The method of dispossession varies from case to case and various methods usually coexist. The imperialist state often resorted to direct force for dispossessing the peasants of the colonized state of their land and natural resources. It appeared primarily as a conflict of the colonizer state against the colonized people and gave birth to anti-colonial struggles and emergent nationalism. The nature of colonial exploitation varied. It supplemented or substituted direct force and extraction whenever necessary with a colonial revenue and trading system. Extensive rural indebtedness and a structural deficit in international trade were often the result. And yet, rural indebtedness of the direct producers has continued to be an important method of alienating land from the peasants in post-colonial times. 'Primitive accumulation' by which the state redefines rights to land to dispossess the peasantry was yet another route of colonial expropriation but the situation had to change with independence and the establishment of a democratic political system in India. The question remains in what ways dispossession still continues.

In the multi-party democracy of modern India land acquisition using state power under various legal and semi-legal guises has become the dominant method in recent years. In this respect it bears resemblance to the method of 'primitive accumulation' described by Marx (1977). However, important variations have been introduced particularly on account of a multi-party democratic system and the pre-existence of a developed capitalist class. Private as well as communal land and related common property resources are acquired by the state for 'public purpose'. They are increasingly being transferred to private corporations on terms favourable to them, at times in the guise of 'public private partnership' to stimulate growth and development. In this context 'land' can be used as a reasonable proxy for most natural resources because almost all significant common property resources like common village land, forests, mountains, rivers, water bodies, coast lines, underground mineral resources, etc require access to land in some way. Legally land acquisition and dispossession proceed by diluting or denying both individual and communal property rights to land in 'public interest' through successive revisions of the Land Acquisition Act.[2] In more extreme cases the land is simply acquired by blatantly bending laws with the compliance of the government. In this respect the primary role of the state has not been to promote efficient working of the price mechanism in the land market; instead its actions tend to suppress the price mechanism through land acquisition at bureaucratically decided arbitrary prices. False, indefinitely delayed or partially implemented compensation price and procedures full of bureaucratic harassments for the ordinary peasants leaves the system open to manipulations at every step.

In the developmental politics that is played out in this context, laws for acquisition are enacted to suit 'public purpose' defined by the state and, presented as compulsions for achieving higher economic growth needed by even those who are being dispossessed. As the state intervenes to acquire land for promoting development, the old Ricardian conflict between the landlords and the capitalists makes its appearance but with the difference that the 'landlords' in this case are usually small peasants and tenants. And, the zone of conflict gets much wider drawing in many more poor people mostly in the countryside who depend for their livelihood on agriculture and common property resources. In addition to ordinary cultivating peasants, they may be tenants and agricultural workers, fishermen, boatmen or vegetable cart-pullers. They all derive a meagre livelihood based on transporting agricultural produce to local markets. In particularly arid areas they may be nomadic tribal with animal husbandry as their sole livelihood and for many forest dwellers it may be forest rather than cultivated land that may provide the main source of livelihood. In this way the zone of the conflict of dispossession becomes wider and, a confrontation between the state and ordinary poor people in the countryside over land acquisition gathers momentum.

'Land' as a general proxy for natural resources has an apparently paradoxical aspect. It often appears that less land is required for the same activity in the modern sector in urban areas. For instance, high-rise urban dwelling, urban markets or malls save space compared to similar activities in rural areas. This impression is misleading because the supporting supply lines of power, water and other infrastructure need land indirectly in such activities. Electricity generation would require hydroelectric power from dams on rivers; mines for coal for thermal power, iron ore, bauxite for construction and machinery occupying land not only in mining areas but also requiring transport facilities; similarly food processing, coastal fishing need transport and even refrigeration facilities which in turn require electricity. Such examples can be multiplied. These indirect requirements are in addition to land needed for direct activities and facilities in urban areas like roads, transit system, bridges and so on which in turn require coal, iron, etc. Together they usually add up to considerably higher natural resource intensity per unit of output in industrial production, especially in urban areas amounting to more land needed indirectly to save land directly.[3]

Use of land as a composite proxy for all natural resources implies that a variety of livelihoods are destroyed in the natural sector when land is acquired for industry. And yet, a development strategy that is premised on the assumption that the 'investment climate' for private corporations needs to be improved by transferring land in their favour implies that a variety of livelihoods connected with land must be destroyed first as the 'cost of development'. And yet, this is no more than a consequence of the standard assumption that improving the climate for private investment has to be the central piece of development strategy (Kalecki, 1943). It has shaped conservative fiscal policy by tending to downplay the role of public investment and nationalized industry; encourages a hostile attitude towards government spending on social welfare and budget deficit to leave more opportunity for the private sector and supports privatization the dogma of 'sound finance' to reduce budget deficit. Intervention by the state to acquire land for 'public purpose' should appear as a paradox in such a conservative fiscal regime. And yet the paradox vanishes when it is realized that the aim of the 'public purpose' is to improve climate for private investment. The mechanism that is put in place for this purpose is to hand over the acquired land acquired at an arbitrarily low price to large private business and corporations as incentives for them to invest. This is often accompanied by almost free water, electricity, road connectivity and other infrastructural facilities partially or wholly provided by the state. In addition, usual tax and fiscal incentives are used to encourage private investment, particularly in infrastructure.

Nevertheless, even under the best of circumstances the climate for investment particularly in long gestation projects take considerable time to improve. In the meantime, creation of adequate new employment in place of the livelihoods destroyed becomes the most vulnerable point of this strategy. Although jobs created in the corporate sector with highly mechanized and automated technology have higher labour productivity in relation to wage, the surplus per worker is higher and effective demand determining the size of the market usually proves to be a barrier to absorbing all the displaced labour. Since expansionary fiscal policy and higher public investment are discouraged in the conservative fiscal regime, neither private nor public consumption demand expands sufficiently. At the same time, foreign trade fails to provide an escape route to deficiency in demand, except for a handful of fortunate countries that succeed in achieving sufficient export surplus to offset the limitation of the size of the domestic market (India is not one of the fortunate ones with import exceeding export with current account deficit in most years). As the incentive for private investment tends to weaken against the barrier of insufficient demand, it becomes all the more important for the government to overcome the problem of demand deficiency not by increasing public investment in this conservative fiscal climate, but by providing investment incentives to private business through cheap access to land and related natural resources.[4]

Providing favourable access to land and natural resources in this way to large corporations and industrial houses has negative repercussions on traditional employment and livelihood because, on balance it destroys more livelihood than it creates employment. And yet, its impact on growth of output may turn out to be favourable in so far as total output from higher productivity of those employed in the corporate sector outweighs the loss of output through dispossession in the traditional sector. This is a scenario for jobless growth; GDP records high growth but employment and opportunities for livelihood may dwindle. Schumpeter's vision of capitalism as a continuous process of creative destruction comes into play in a grim way as the destruction of livelihoods of the number dispossessed continuously out-paces the creation of new jobs through corporate-led industrial development. Unemployment grows along with output and, the more the government tries to reduce unemployment and demand deficiency by raising the incentive to invest through transferring land and other natural resources, the greater becomes the number of those dispossessed without jobs. It operates like a trap in which an increasing number of displaced people are caught.

Along with the growing imbalance of unemployment in the labour market, another imbalance typically arises in the market for natural resources related to land. While productivity of labour is higher, the direct and indirect natural resource intensity per unit of output is also higher in the corporate sector on account of both the nature of the technology used and the types of goods produced. In addition, large corporate industries have as prerequisites large infrastructural investments in economic and social overheads. This intensifies the hunt for natural resources leading to destruction of nature, forests, mountains, rivers and coastlines. Traditional tribal and rural communities who do not have a strong political 'voice' and often live in areas exceptionally rich in natural resources become particularly vulnerable. The traditional escape route for industrialization in the age of imperialism was to externalize the hunt for natural resources as far as possible by extending the reach of the imperial power in the colonies. With the passing of that age, newly industrializing populous countries like China or India have more limited options usually in even less developed regions, and turn to a form of internal colonization of their own poor citizens in natural resource rich areas.

The continuous creation of a surplus labour from destroyed livelihood in the traditional sector does not necessarily create unlimited supply of labour at a constant real wage rate available from the traditional sector (Lewis,1954). Instead of being a process of creation of wage labour from a passive reservoir of labour in the traditional economy, this destructive process tends to alter both the form and the content of supply of labour. In the migration that occurs to urban industrial areas, individuals or families mostly do not work as part of the regular industrial work force but rather coexist uneasily with it competing for the same urban space. Because they have been largely 'pushed' away from the traditional sector and not 'pulled' by expectation of higher wages in the modern industrial sector, they are forced to eke out an existence wherever they can and, in whatever way possible in economic conflict and cooperation with the organized sector. Their earning opportunities vary enormously depending on the circumstances. The outcome is a proliferating informal sector characterized by a diverse range of economic activities and labour forms defying easy characterization. Nevertheless, three features seem relatively common.

First, the unit of labour used for production is often different from wage labour in factory employment. 'Self-employment' is a prominent form where the whole or part of the family including children constitutes a composite unit of labour. Generally this entails longer hours of work for the family unit as a whole with earning per hour per person much lower compared to that of wage labour; but total earning of the family at times may be higher. But unlike with wage labour no valid distinction between profit and wage is meaningful; nor is it meaningful in these cases to compare productivity of the worker in the formal sector with the productivity of a family unit without normalizing the labour unit.

Second, many in the informal sector who are not self-employed, do not often have a single employer. They combine several different part-time occupations with different employers on different terms. Some might also combine part-time self-employment with contract wage labour. Assigning 'principal status' to the nature of their occupation is problematic in all such cases, e.g. time disposition by different occupations might differ substantially from the income earned from those occupations.

Third, the 'legality' of their occupation is often in question without proper legal entitlement to resources. Bribes and side payments in various forms are recurring cost for access to resources which depresses net earnings substantially in many occupations.

Most of those joining the informal sector in urban and semi-urban areas as part of an unorganized labour force live in illegal shanty towns. They try to have urban facilities like electricity, water supplies, schools, hospitals to which they are often not considered legally entitled especially without a permanent address. Yet their economic activities depend crucially on their access to urban economic infrastructures like water, electricity and transport. While as illegal occupants in urban areas, they may not have legal access to some of these urban facilities they cannot survive without them. Illegality becomes an unavoidable compulsion of the situation as it gives rise to the strange spectacle of a large number of citizens of a democratic country being forced to make a living by breaking laws![5] Not surprisingly it gives the 'law and order' machinery a special, often arbitrary power to threaten and blackmail them at will, while a relatively new brand of politicians make their entry into democratic politics as 'service providers'. They work through the labyrinth of legality, illegality and bureaucracy as go-between agents, bribe givers as well as bribe takers, responsible for providing these services. At the same time, another class of agents emerges in areas where land has been acquired. They act as agents dealing with purchase, lease or sale of land in various capacities and, operate in large numbers particularly in real estate development as middlemen for housing complexes, shops, malls, private schools and other allied activities. An array of lawyers also finds this business lucrative. In this maze of legality and illegality the law-enforcing machinery gets entangled with the new politics of patronage that develops around land acquired by the government for public purposes but intended for private profit.[6] Some more successful service providers have been known to achieve prominence in local politics and graduate to higher levels by having the power to bend rules for their supporters and even by enacting and amending laws. In such situations the distinction between illegal and legal corruption begins to disappear fast.

The relation between the formal and the informal sector often turns out to be ambiguous, a mixture of conflict and cooperation. For instance, in some cases they may compete in the market for final product and infrastructure facilities, but have a mutually beneficial cooperative relation in terms of sub-contracting arrangements for inputs or labour contracts. These relations are difficult to generalize as they vary from enterprise to enterprise. Nevertheless, competition over urban space, infrastructure and natural resource availability are sufficiently general features that seem to dominate the overall scene. In this respect the growth of the informal sector affects adversely the productivity of the corporate sector by contesting for resources in short supply. Ironically however the corporate sector grows at the same time by contributing to the expansion of the informal sector through dispossession. This almost ironic pattern of inter-dependence becomes the characteristic feature of development by dispossession.

A typical outcome of absorbing labour displaced by dispossession into the informal sector is steady deterioration of urban facilities, quality of life and pollution on account of over-crowding and congestion by so-called 'illegal' users of urban space and infrastructure. External diseconomies of various kinds arise through congestion and infrastructure bottlenecks in so far as organized large business sector is concerned. Irregular supply of power and water, transport bottlenecks resulting in delays that upset regular production and delivery schedule; poor housing, sanitary conditions and pollution cause ill health and absenteeism of workers. These factors contribute to depressing labour productivity below its technologically feasible level in the corporate sector. Acute infrastructural bottlenecks are lamented loudly by corporate lobbies and seen as a major hurdle to improving the investment climate. The typical response of the government is to intensify attempts at land acquisition in support of the strategy of corporate-led growth which aggravates the problem further.

The urban problems are accelerated by growing rural distress. Those among the dispossessed left behind in rural areas are often too young or too old, without any experience of outside life, isolated spatially or linguistically. They are the most vulnerable, sacrificed at the altar of corporate-led development with their means of livelihood destroyed as land, river, forest, coast line and other common property resources are acquired by the government and large businesses. Common grazing land begins to disappear, reducing viability of raising animals in villages to supplement income and threatens many nomadic groups with extinction in arid areas. Agricultural communities lose their livelihood due to diversion of land to mining, pollution of water bodies and construction of dams on rivers for hydroelectric power. In any case the electricity generated is seldom meant for them, but is needed to supply power to large industries and cities. Traditional fishing communities are threatened as coasts are taken over by large-scale mechanized fishing and big hotels catering to the tourist industry. Reduced access to forest products and dwindling forest land snatch away the meagre livelihoods of forest dwellers. Forest dwelling population lose on an average around one-third of their meagre income. With less land, water and other natural resources like forests available villagers are forced to survive by diversifying their sources of livelihood through non-agricultural activities. In a way it becomes a mirror image as the importance of the informal sector increases in the rural economy.[7]

Intensification of the drive to capture land either by the government or the corporations does not necessarily mean that more land would be used for industrial development. The profit motive of private corporations determines how to use the land they acquire for public purpose. This usually results in violating or bending laws, e.g. through illegal mining, exports of minerals meant for domestic use, diversion of land earmarked for industry to real estates, etc. Often the route to highest profit is simply leaving the acquired land unutilized for future capital gains or selling mineral products through various option schemes in future markets by leaving it under the ground for long periods. It amounts to sitting on mineral deposits or preventing its full exploitation contradicting the stated purpose of raising the growth rate. A significant amount of transferred land to corporations remains unutilized for these reasons often in the face of acute shortage of natural resources.[8]

Nevertheless, even as only a fraction of transferred land is used for corporate-led industrialization, transferring land and natural resources to private corporations becomes one of the most potent political weapons promoting both inequality and intra-corporate rivalry for land grab. It forges mutual dependence between the state and selected capitalists as the biggest source of massive transfer of wealth in favour of politically favoured corporations, a particular version of 'crony capitalism' around allocation of land and natural resources by the state. It also becomes the main base of policy-induced corruption and huge scams. This corruption is not just illegal and personal, but legal and systemic, because it stems from deliberate twists to policy given by the government to promote selected corporate interests and justified in the name of improving the investment climate. Ironically, the climate for investment gets corrupted too in this process. Corporations seize the opportunity not to make profit through production, but follow a quicker and more effective route to acquire wealth through grabbing land. This form of corruption corrodes the system of governance as it involves players at several levels, the political class formulating policies for land acquisition, the bureaucracy in charge of implementing them and, the politically favoured corporations as the main promoter of this policy as well as its potential beneficiaries. In this arrangement of mutualism the corporations return the favour not merely at a personal level by bribing concerned politicians and bureaucrats but raise to the higher level of systemic corruption of policies by using a general strategy of making handsome donations to political parties of all colours, and more donations to their favoured party and politician. As the compromised political class and obedient bureaucrats become accomplices for enacting, implementing and bending land acquisition laws and policies, the distinction between making profit from production and accumulating wealth through land grab with the help of state power begins to disappear. Dispossession of the poor from land continues primarily for transferring wealth to the corporations and industrial development of the country becomes incidental to this process, a mere side show.

In the competitive electoral game of multi-party democracy, no party wants to be left handicapped in collecting funds for elections. Land and natural resource policies of every government in power are influenced heavily by this consideration. While in opposition all political parties tend to take a critical stance, in power they fall in line quickly under similar compulsions. The result is a growing disconnect between the vast majority of people threatened with dispossession and destruction of livelihood based on land and, the elected representatives of the people in the government. The growing gulf between them has to be managed in a poor people's democracy of one adult one vote by changing the content of representation, but keeping the form. This is done by relying more and more on the power of corporate oligarchy. Their contributions to the election funds of political parties help to massively raise electoral expenditures. The 'entry price' to the race of election is raised to serve as a barrier to the possibility of direct political representation by ordinary citizens. Corporate contribution through paid advertisements in media operates as a powerful supporting device in manipulating public opinion in elections. An increasing number of big industrialists or their agents enter directly the parliament by securing tickets in exchange for handsome donations to fight elections under the banner of various political parties They become 'representatives of the people' in a 'free and fair' election to deal with the problem of 'land acquisition'. Popular resistance to it is made as far invisible as is possible by the corporate-sponsored media, and all political parties take up the issue while in opposition half-heartedly with too many skeletons in their own cupboards.

In this process of development by dispossession, big business not only transforms the nature of political representation in a democracy, but undergoes significant transformation itself. The focus shifts from making profit in production to land grab facilitated by the government. Traditional trade unions and labour movements are increasingly at a loss with the major source of profit shifting from exploitation of workers on the factory floor to the far more profitable business of land grabbing. Competition operates less fiercely for increasing market shares in products, but fiercely in cultivating the government for the favour of allotment of land based resources. New entrants do better at times in this competition than the traditional heavyweights in the corporate sector because of their political closeness to the ruling power. They are elevated to the class of extremely rich in a short time as they are especially favoured for acquiring wealth through land transfer. Such quick transition to the extremely rich elite would have been impossible through gradual accumulation of profit from production. India has had one of the largest increases in the number of dollar billionaires in the world in recent years. Their number increased from 8 to 52 in less than a decade. Many among these newly emerged 'individuals of exceptional net worth' are connected with transfer of land and natural resources (Gandhi and Walton, 2012). Privatization by undervaluing assets of state enterprises had been a major route to creating overnight billionaires in Russia in recent years. The Indian way has been promoting land grab in the name of higher growth, the politics of 'growthmanship'. And yet, the irony of the situation is unmistakable .The investment climate has to be perverted thoroughly by making private land grab with the help of state power far more profitable than production.

Notes

1. Although the expression, 'development by dispossession' is borrowed from Harvey (2004), our focus is closer to Marx's(1977) original formulation about dispossession from land and related livelihood. In contrast Harvey discusses many other methods of dispossession like privatization of public sector undertakings, imposition of financial claims, etc.
2. The 'eminent domain' clause (1894) established the sovereign right of the colonial Indian state on land. It coexists uneasily with private or communal property right and has undergone (and is undergoing) successive revisions trying to define the right of the state to acquire land for 'public purpose'.
3. The ratio of land that is indirectly used for saving a unit of land would be a useful measure. It is analogous to direct to indirect labour measured in mainstream theory by the labour/capital ratio. On the computation of indirect land used see also note 9.
4. The politics of improving private 'investment climate' rather than higher public investment for countering business cycles was recognized early (1943) as the main thrust of conservative strategy by Kalecki in 'Political Aspects of Full Employment' (1971, original 1943).
5. Sanyal (2006) analyzed the role played by the informal sector in capitalistic development in modern times, while Chatterjee (2011) examined its political consequences especially for Indian demcracy.
6. Levien (2012) provides an analytical description of this process based on field survey.
7. In India in 1951 about 72 per cent were cultivators and 28 per cent agricultural labourers. In 2011, 45 per cent were cultivators and 55 per cent landless labourers. With decreasing size of average land holding, more people seek partial or total livelihood outside and dispossessed population only add to this vague category of non-agricultural rural sector which is estimated to absorb around 3/4ths of the increase in rural labour force.
8. Although no firm estimate of unutilized land is available, some observers from different areas put it between 40 to 60 per cent in private discussions particularly in SEZ (Special Economic Zone) areas.

References

1. P. Chatterjee, 2011. *Lineages of the Political Society: Studies in Post-Colonial Democracy*, Columbia University Press, pp. 22–24.
2. A. Gandhi and Walton 2012. 'Where do Indian billionaires get their wealth', *Economic and Political Weekly*, October 6, Vol. XLVII, No. 40.
3. D. Harvey, 2003. *The New Imperialism*, Oxford University Press, Oxford, p. 144.
4. Kalecki, M. 1971. 'Political Business Cycles' in his *Selected Essays in the Dynamics of the Capitalist Economy*, Cambridge University Press, Cambridge.
5. K. Marx, 1977. *Capital*, see especially Vol. 1, Part 7, Ch. 26, and *Selected Works*, Vol. 2, Progress Publishers, Moscow.
6. R. Dorfman, P. Samuelson and R. Solow, 1958. *Linear Programming and Economic Analysis*, Chapters 9, 10.
7. L. Pasinetti, 1977. *Lectures on the Theory of Production*, Columbia University Press, New York.
8. K. Sanyal, 2007. *Rethinking Capitalist Development: Primitive Accumulation, Governmentality and Post-colonial Capitalism*, Routledge, London.
9. J. Robinson, 1974. History versus Equilibrium, Thames Paper on Political Economy, Autumn.
10. R. Harrod, 1939. 'An Essay in Dynamic Theory', *Economic Journal*, March.
11. A. Bhaduri, 1985. 'Capitalist Accumulation in Logical and Historical Time', Economie Appliquee, No. 2 (in French translation; original later published in *Economic and Political Weekly*, Special Number, 1985 Vol. 20, pp. 1903–7).
12. W. Leontief, 1986. *Input-Output Economics*, 2nd edition, Oxford University Press, New York.
13. A. Lewis, 1954. 'Economic Development with Unlimited Supplies of labour', *Manchester School of Economic and Social Studies*, Vol. 22, pp. 139-91.
14. J. Schumpeter, 1944. *Capitalism, Socialism and Democracy*, George Allen and Unwin, London.

6

A Formal Model of Development by Dispossession

Part I: A Model

The main arguments of Chapter 4 may be schematized starkly in a formal model to draw out some analytical implications. Two assumptions will be made mostly for expositional simplicity.

(a) No distinction will be made between the organized industrial sector and its corporate sub-sector. They are lumped together as having the common characteristic of productivity per worker higher than in the traditional natural economy from which people are being dispossessed and displaced. The natural sector includes not only small peasants, tenants but persons who derive livelihoods in numerous ways from land, river, water bodies, forest, mountains and coastlines through activities like small scale transport of agricultural produce, collection of minor forest products, fishing, animal husbandry, ferrying, sand collection from river beds, etc.

(b) We assume an 'equilibrium' situation as the initial condition. It allows us to focus on (discrete) changes in the relevant variables brought about by land acquisition. The reader is reminded throughout (until equation15) that we are dealing with perturbation from an equilibrium by retaining the awkward sign of discrete increment (Δ) from initial equilibrium. Thus the formalism deals with 'flows' during a period while the corresponding 'stocks' inherited at the beginning of the period are assumed to be in equilibrium. This device is essential to keep out the 'arbitrariness' of disequilibrium conditions in initial stocks which can affect the consequences of a given perturbation differently. As a simple illustration, the difference between mass unemployment and shortage of labour as given initial conditions would have very different consequences for a given level of perturbation by dispossession and displacement. To put somewhat dramatically, the assumption of equilibrium as initial condition keeps out the arbitrary intrusion of 'history' into formal modelling (Robinson, 1974; Bhaduri,1985).

Let n and c be subscripts for the natural and the corporate (or organized) sector respectively, and x_j be their respective labour productivity of sector j(j = c, n). If ΔL_n is the number of labour dispossessed from the natural sector and, ΔL_c the number employed in the corporate sector, the changes in net output and employment caused by dispossession becomes,

(1) $(x_c\Delta L_c - x_n\Delta L_n) = X$, with $x_c > x_n$ by assumption.

$X > 0$ implies growth of output, $X = 0$ implies stagnation, while $X < 0$ means decline in output. The proportional positive, zero or negative growth rate of output, $g = [(x_c\Delta L_c - x_n\Delta L_n)/(x_n\Delta L_n)]$ span a wide range. If all dispossessed workers from the natural sector are employed in the corporate sector without any time lag, $\Delta L_c = \Delta L_n$, and the rate of growth of output is at its maximum, $g_{max} = [(x_c/x_n) - 1]$ with no unemployment. If none of the dispossessed find employment, $\Delta L_c = 0$ in (2) and the rate of growth is at its minimum, $g_{min} = -1$ with unemployment at its maximum. In actual situations to be analysed the growth rate would typically lie between these logical extremes.

The full employment model of maximum growth with all the labour reallocated from the low productivity natural to the high productivity corporate sector is a favourite of conservative economists celebrated under the Schumpeterian banner of 'creative destruction' under capitalism. And yet, it is a most unlikely occurrence during a short period for two reasons. First, there is the problem of market size or effective demand. For instance, if the corporate productivity is three times higher (an under-estimate) than in the natural sector, the size of the market has to be three times larger (other things equal) to absorb the output produced by the corporate sector. This can hardly happen through expansion of the domestic market in the short period and leaving out exceptionally successful export surplus countries (and India has not been one of them), the external market can hardly do the job. Moreover, it is a zero sum game in which for every export surplus country there would be an import surplus case.

Apart from deficient demand, there is also the problem of the time-scale. Reallocation of labour from the natural to the corporate sector is an extended process due to various frictions in reallocation or 'frictional unemployment'. The time horizon permitted by the electoral politics in a democracy is hardly sufficient for this. The pressure of those displaced without jobs in the corporate sector mounts leading to forced expansion of the informal sector. Thus in a typical situation to be analysed during any short period, some of the dispossessed find employment in the corporate sector, some are unemployed and survive by joining the informal sector and a few are totally marginalized destitute. And yet, there may be some growth in output.

In addition to the problem of unemployment, development by dispossession faces another critical issue. Land and many related natural resources cannot be produced within the industrial system but needs to be acquired for raising corporate production. In a linear production system of fixed coefficients, the direct and indirect land requirement (like labour) may be computed approximately through the Leontief inverse matrix of the input output table under certain assumptions.[1] Let, a_j be the amount of land related natural resource directly and indirectly required per unit of output. Consequently,

(2) $a_j x_j = k_j$ = direct and indirect land or natural resource requirement per unit of labour employed in sector j.

Using (1) and (2) the natural resource balance relation resulting from dispossession and development is given as,

(3) $k_c\Delta L_c - k_n\Delta L_n = K$, where $K > 0$, indicates excess demand, $K = 0$ indicates exact balance and, $K < 0$ indicates excess supply of natural resource or land.

A simple arithmetical example based on (1) to (3) illustrates a typical configuration of employment and natural resource.

	Corporate Sector	Natural Sector
Employment	$\Delta L_c = +4$	$\Delta L_n = -10$
Labour productivity	$x_c = 6$	$x_n = 2$
Output gain and loss	$x_c\Delta L_c = 6.4 = 24$	$x_n\Delta L_n = 2(-10) = -20$
Natural resource per unit of output	$a_c = 2$,	$a_n = 0.50$
Natural resource per unit of labour	$a_c x_c = k_c = 12$	$a_n x_n = k_j = 1$

The configuration above implies, growth rate in output of $(24 - 20)/20 = 20\%$ and decline in employment of $(4 - 10)/(10) = -60\%$. Given the productivity ratio, $(x_c/x_n) = 10/4 = 2.5$ g output level will remain unchanged so long as 250 persons are dispossessed for each 100 employed in the corporate sector, i.e. productivity ratio is inversely related to the ratio of corporate employment to dispossessed persons. If productivity of the corporate sector is higher than 2.5 times that of the natural sector, say $(6/2) = 3$ as in the above table, it would mean unemployment with positive growth of output, while a ratio lower than 2.5, say $(3/2) = 1.5$ would mean negative growth in output with unemployment. Total natural resource needed by the corporate sector from (3) is, $k_c\Delta L_c = 12.4 = 48$ while natural resource made available through dispossession in the natural sector $= k_n\Delta L_n = (1).10 = 10$. Therefore, in this example $(10 - 4) = 6$ unemployed persons is coupled with excess demand for land related natural resource of $(10 - 48) = -38$ units. This double deficit, in employment creation and in natural resource availability appears typical of corporate-led development by dispossession.

Dispossessed from the natural sector without alternative employment in the corporate sector, the uprooted population strives to eke out an existence in where ever they can. The outcome is a diverse range of economic activities that are fused together in the informal sector. Let ΔL_i stand for labour engaged and k_i for land-related natural resource required per worker in the informal sector. Incorporating the natural resource requirement of the informal sector (3) is revised as,

(4) $k_c\Delta L_c + k_i\Delta L_i - k_n\Delta L_n = N$. In this extended equation incorporating the informal sector $N > 0, = 0$ and < 0 correspond to excess demand, exact balance or excess supply of natural resources.

Under the assumption of equilibrium in employment as initial condition, there is no inherited stock of unemployment. This sets an upper bound to employment in the informal sector as,

(5) $\Delta L_i = h.(\Delta L_n - \Delta L_c),\ 1 \geq h \geq 0,$

If h is less than unity, those who are unable to join even the informal sector become the extreme destitute rejected even by the informal sector. They are the 'sacrifices' offered at the alter of corporate led development. However, for simplicity of exposition we would ignore these extreme cases of destitution and assume $h = 1$, i.e. all the dispossessed persons not employed in the corporate sector somehow find refuse in the informal sector.[2]

In normal circumstances, augmentation of the labour force through the informal sector would produce more output but would also make excess demand for natural resources even more acute. Paradoxically however the expansion of the informal sector often also has an unintended effect of reducing the natural resource imbalance by reducing the productivity in the corporate sector.[14] This operates typically through 'congestion' and over-crowding created especially in urban housing, transports, power, water and several other economic and social infrastructural facilities. The deteriorating quality of life and pollution regretted by the more privileged urban sections impacts on labour productivity in the corporate sector through increase in absenteeism and late arrivals (due to frequency of illness, traffic congestion, etc), disruption of power and water supply from time to time or irregular supply of inputs. They combine to reduce productivity from its technologically feasible maximum (q). We represent this negative effect of congestion on corporate productivity by the following specific function,

(6) $(x_c/q) = [1/[1 + (k_i\Delta L_i/k_c\Delta L_c)]$

Equation (6) specifies how realised productivity x_c decreases from its technologically feasible maximum q, as the ratio of the natural resource requirement of informal $(k_i\Delta L_i)$ to that of the corporate sector $(k_c\Delta L_c)$ increases from some negligible (zero) to some arbitrarily large positive number. It captures how the congestion effect arising from claim made on natural resources by the informal sector in relation to the formal sector operate as a multiplicative fraction reducing corporate labour productivity from its feasible maximum (q)

At h = 1, we obtain from (6),

(7) $x_c = q[k_c\Delta L_c/(k_c\Delta L_c + k_i\Delta L_i)]$

If natural resource demand and supply are in strict balance, equality holds, N = 0 in (4) and using this in (7), we obtain,

(8) $x_c = q[(k_c\Delta L_c/k_n\Delta L_n)]$, at h=1 and N=0.

Equation (8) represents an equilibrium locus characterized by the sufficiently reduced value of x_c in relation to q at which all open unemployment is disguised by expansion of the informal sector (i.e. h = 1) and demand and supply of natural resource is in exact balance, i.e. N = 0)

We could rewrite (8) also as,

(9) $\Delta L_c = w.\Delta Ln$, where $w = (k_n/k_c^{max})$, and $k_c^{max} = a_c q$, i.e., the maximum natural resource requirement per unit of output of the corporate sector when its labour productivity is at its feasible maximum q. Since $k_c^{max} > k_n$, the straight line on the ΔLn and ΔL_c plane is a ray ON passing through the origin with a slope necessarily less than tan 45° (see Diagram 1). It represents the locus of equilibrium configurations of natural resource balance at

different levels of dispossession, ΔL_n and employment offered by the corporate sector ΔL_c. Thus each point of this locus corresponds to a level of dispossession releasing natural resource to the corporate sector. When it is forced to share this with the informal sector with no open unemployment (h = 1) causing congestion and overcrowding, an awkward balance between demand and supply of natural resources (N = 0) might occur in some circumstances with reduction in corporate labour productivity.

The ray ON depicting equation (9) for supply side balance for natural resources is misleadingly incomplete without specifying how the level of corporate employment (ΔL_c) is determined. For instance, we had arbitrarily assumed that the level of corporate employment is arbitrarily given in the previous arithmetical example (in which 4 out of 10 dispossessed labourers found corporate employment).The level of employment which the corporate sector can offer is demand determined, i.e. aggregate demand constrains the level of corporate output and employment. To specify the demand constraint in the model, we assume, b_j = investment required per unit of output in sector j (j = c, i, n). Thus total increase in investment of the corporate and informal sector on account of land acquisition is given by,

(10) $\Delta I = \{b_c x_c \Delta L_c + b_i x_i \Delta L_i\} + \Delta I_g$ where, $b_j x_j$ = investment per unit of labour in sector j and ΔI_g =investment related to land acquisition by the government.

Assuming fixed sectoral propensities to save (s_j), the savings of the economy is given as,

(11) $\Delta S = (s_c x_c \Delta L_c + s_i x_i \Delta L_i - s_n x_n \Delta L_n) + \Delta S_g$, where ΔS_g = savings by the government especially from on account of land, and $(-s_n x_n \Delta L_n)$ is the dis-saving by the natural sector due to dispossession.

Only for expositional simplicity we would assume (perhaps not too unreasonably) that the dis-saving due to dispossession of the natural sector is balanced by the saving of the informal sector, i.e.

(12) $(s_i x_i \Delta L_i - s_n x_n \Delta L_n) = 0$

Equality of investment (ΔI) and saving (ΔS) determines output through aggregate demand in the corporate and the informal sector. From (10), (11) and (12), $\Delta I = \Delta S$ implies,

(13) $[(b_c x_c \Delta L_c + b_i x_i \Delta L_i) - (s_c x_c \Delta L_c)] + G = 0, G = (\Delta I_g - \Delta S_g)$

At h = 1, this is rewritten as,

(14) $u \,.\, \Delta L_n + v = \Delta Lc$, $u = \{b_i x_i / [s_c x_c - (b_c x_c + b_i x_i)]\}$, $v = G/[s_c x_c - (b_c x_c + b_i x_i)]$.

The close analogy with Keynesian income determination model for the corporate sector can be made more explicit by noting that $x_c \Delta L_c$ and $x_i \Delta L_i$ in the investment function (10) should be interpreted as expected levels of output at normal capacity utilization (Harrod, 1939), while its equality with saving in (11) ensures that this expected level is realised because the size of the market is just adequate to absorb that level of output. The sign of the square bracketed term in the denominator, $[s_c x_c - (b_c x_c + b_i x_i)]$ in (14) may be assumed positive in so far as it satisfies the usual one variable Keynesian income adjustment stability condition that saving is more responsive than investment to change in output (per worker). This is more easily seen by rearranging terms in (13) to yield,

$\Delta Lc = (b_i x_i \Delta L_i + G)/(s_c x_c - b_c x_c)$, where the denominator is the so called multiplier when both saving and investment depend on income in determining corporate employment with the additional condition that all dispossessed workers who could not find employment in the corporate sector are absorbed in the informal sector, i.e. h = 1, $\Delta L_i = (\Delta L_n - \Delta L_c)$.

Equation (14) shows the demand determined level of corporate employment ΔLc that is consistent with the level of land acquisition and dispossession ΔL_n carried out by the government. On the other hand, equation (9) shows the corporate level of employment ΔLc at a reduced labour productivity due to congestion cost that is consistent with the available supply of natural resources through dispossession. The interaction between (9) and (14) captures corporate employment proceeds with land acquisition. The resulting dynamics may or may not have an 'equilibrium' or rest point which would be stable only under certain conditions. We may represent it heuristically in the following Diagram 1 where ON represents equation (9). AD represents equation (14) assuming that the intercept is negative, G < 0 with government saving exceeding government investment on account of land acquisition.

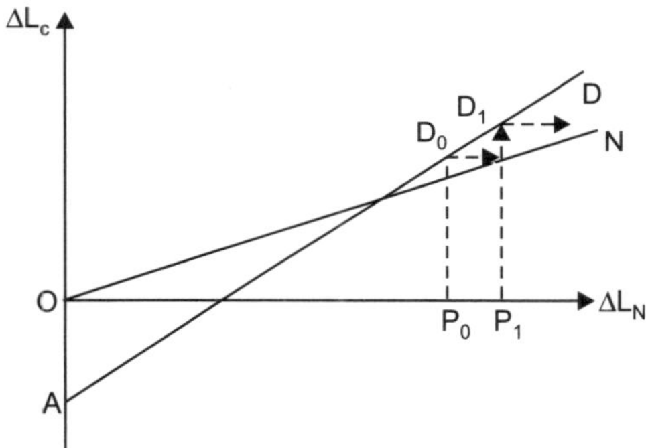

Diagram 1: Unstable

The discrete dynamics presented above works in the following way. At an initial level of land acquisition P_0 along the horizontal axis, the demand determined level of corporate output is D_0 which necessitates land acquisition P_1 maintaining natural resource balance to make this level of output feasible from the supply side. However, this pushes up demand determined corporate employment further to D_1 which in turn raises further the demand of natural resources. The equilibrium is assumed to exist at the intersection of the two lines in the positive quadrant at point E but is clearly unstable because the slope of AD is greater than the slope of ON. However, reversing simply the inequalities of the slopes is not enough to restore equilibrium because equilibrium would not exist (Diagram 3) . It would exist only if along with the reversal of slopes the intercept OA is also positive (Diagram 2). The existence and uniqueness of equilibrium and its stability are interlinked properties well known for simple linear systems.

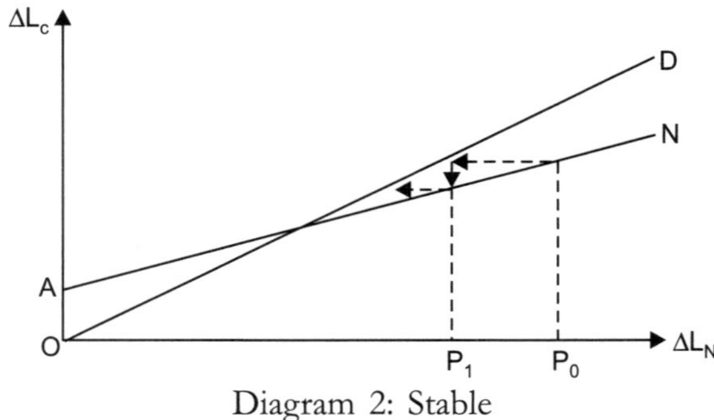

Diagram 2: Stable

A more exact analysis of stability linking up properties of existence with stability of equilibrium is simpler to conduct in continuous time. Since both natural resource balance in (9) and employment offered by the corporate sector in (14) are functions of the level of dispossession $\Delta L_{s,}$ dispossession becomes the adjusting variable in the dynamics. This is represented by,

(15) $(dl_n/dt) = \theta\ [(u\ .\ l_n + v) - wl_n],\ \theta > 0$

with ΔL_n redefined as continuous variable l_n, and u, v and w given from (14) and (9) respectively.

The general solution of (15) is given as,

(16) $l_n = Ae^{-(w-u)t} + [v/(w\text{-}u)]$, where A is an arbitrary positive constant.

With $l_n(0)$ at $t = 0$, the particular solution becomes,

(17) $\{l_n(0) - [v/(w - u)]\}\ e^{-(w-u)t} + [v/(w - u)]$.

Equation (17) links formally the existence and stability of equilibrium. For the system to be stable $w > u > 0$ with deviation from equilibrium tending to 0 as t tends to infinity, while the economically meaningful positive equilibrium $[v/(w - u)]$ would exist if $v > 0$.

Equation (16) shows that the system is stable if,

(18) $w > u$, i.e. $(k_n/k_c^{max}) > \{b_i x_i/[s_c x_c - (b_c x_c + b_i x_i)]\}$.

This condition is violated in the above diagram making it unstable. It also shows that a positive equilibrium at $[v/(w - u)]$

exists in the stable case only if $v = G/[s_c x_c - (b_c x_c + b_i x_i)] > 0$ which in turn under the Keynesian one variable stability condition for income adjustment requires $(\Delta I_g - \Delta S_g) > 0$ which again was violated in the above diagram to accommodate the existence of a positive equilibrium in the unstable case (Diagram 3).

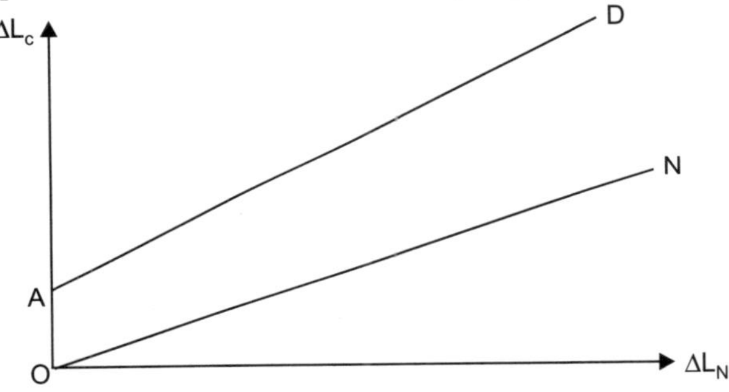

Diagram 3: Non-existence of equilibrium

Some standard comparative static implications follow in the stable case (diagram 2). For instance in only a part of the land made available to the corporations through dispossession is used (1>z>0) and, the rest(1-z) left unused by them for future use(e.g. capital gains) from (8) and (9) the stability condition (18) would reduce to,

(19) zw>u, 1>z>0. This condition may be satisfied for a large enough z and, as a comparative static exercise we confirm the commonsense result,

$(dl_n/dz) = -[wl_n/(zw-u)]$, i.e. use of a higher fraction of land available to the corporations reduces the extent of dispossession in the stable case. However, note from (18) that if corporations hold a sufficiently high fraction of the land for future use (e.g capital gains), z is sufficiently small and the model becomes unstable at the critical value zw = u. This means that if corporations are allowed to hold unused a sufficiently high fraction of land for long, the process of land acquisition would be unstable.

Similarly from (9) it is clear that w decreases with (k_c^{max}) implying from (17) and (18) that sufficiently high natural resource intensive development of the corporate sector is incompatible with stability. In all such unstable cases the process of land and natural resource acquisition may continue to intensify without restoring balance between demand and supply of natural resources.

Finally, the model also hints at the link between land acquisition, corruption and government finance. The positivity of the intercept condition $OA=G>0$ for the existence of a stable, economically meaningful equilibrium in equation (17) as depicted in Diagram 2 suggests that the government needs to invest more than it receives on account of land acquisition. On the other hand, if the government invests relatively little to acquire land, say through low compensation, force and without local consultation, and receives back more from the corporations as its saving, the net balance on account of land operation would turn negative, i.e. $G=(\Delta I_g-\Delta S_g)<0$. This would make land aqquisition a lucrative business for the government but would upset the possibility of the existence of a stable equilibrium. Forcible land acquisition might continue along with growing popular resistance to put the democratic system under increasing pressure.

Part II: Model and Reality: Some Concluding Observations

The model outlined above can be illuminating and misleading at the same time; illuminating in so far as it schematises starkly various inter-connections linking economics with the politics that drives economic growth attempted through in India. However it might also mislead because of its omission of several important aspects. One might say it resembles a cartoon by highlighting crucial features to characterize the situation at the expense of descriptive accuracy.

Perhaps the most important omission of the model is the neglect of ecological implications. The model focuses on the problem of balance between demand for natural resources in the short term by the corporate sector and its supply carried out by dispossession of people from the natural economy which also results in expansion of the informal economy. The longer term ecological implications of achieving demand supply balance is neglected. For instance, irreversible damages to nature which might even render this way of achieving balance impossible in the longer run lie outside the scope of the present analysis. Much like democratic politics itself, the short term tends to overwhelm the long term considerations even if that would not be viable for long.

As an expository device the model specifies an aspect of the investment function in equation (10) for the corporate sector which may be an over-simplification. While it does not undermine the argument that corporate output and employment are constrained by demand, it neglects in particular an important feature namely, a reinforcing tendency in land acquisition by the government. The more the government acquires land on terms highly favourable to corporations and receives in return favour from the corporations, the deeper becomes the nexus between big business and the government. This might strengthen the inclination of the government to acquire more land for the corporations. It is also likely to affect the climate for private investment through labour laws, overt and covert subsidies to the corporate sector etc. Some of these problems were mentioned in Chapter 4 but we were unable to incorporate them satisfactorily in the formalism (except in the discussion of why the model becomes unstable) in this chapter.

It might appear surprising that the model is concerned with land acquisition without referring to the 'land market'. However in reality only a very small fraction of market land is transacted voluntarily in the natural economy based on mutual agreement between the buyer and the seller, partly because small sellers refuse to part with land without alternative possibilities of livelihood and partly because individual buyers cannot get consolidated large area of land without many sellers agreeing more or less simultaneously. Forcible acquisition mostly by the government short-circuits these problems and forecloses options for the development of a land market. Nevertheless, one could have extended the analysis by introducing actual or imputed (relative scarcity) price of land. This might impact on the proportion of land used (parameter z in the model) because the higher the expected price of land is, the lower is likely to be the proportion of land put to current use due to possibility of future capital gains. This happens often when the corporations wait for the 'first move' by the government in creating infrastructure that would raise land price significantly. Analytically, this might also link the parameter z with government investment on land (ΔI_g) which is not explored in the model.

Finally the informal sector enters the analysis as the most important side show of development by dispossession. We assumed for simplicity that all dispossessed people who could not find job in the corporate sector find refuge in the informal sector (h = 1). Relaxing this assumption is formally trivial so long as the value of h is arbitrarily fixed in the open interval ($1 > h > 0$). However, this hardly enriches our understanding till we are able to incorporate the ('push' and 'pull') factors which together influence h. These larger issues remain matters for future research.

Notes

* I am grateful to Duncan Foley, Kaustav Banerjee,Kazimierz Laski, Partha Chatterjee, Rune Skarstein and Srinivas Raghavendra for comments at various stages. Although too numerous to mention, I must also record my debt to numerous activist friends and victims of dispossession who helped me to understand the situation.

1. The Leontief inverse, commonly denoted as $(I\text{-}A)^{-1}$ is an input-output matrix showing direct and indirect requirement of various commodities (as circulating capital) in producing outputs gives a measure so long as various services from land are considered as current input. As an input non-produced in the system this computation is similar to that in the labour theory of value but its purpose is very different in the present context. See Dorfman, Samuelson and Solow (1953) for an elementary introduction and Pasinetti (1981).
2. In a stationary state of output $x_c\Delta L_c + x_i(\Delta L_n - \Delta L_c) - x_n\Delta L_n = 0$, h = 1, which reduces to, $(x_c - x_i)\Delta L_c = (x_n - x_i)\Delta L_n$. So long as the corporate sector has the highest labour productivity, the left hand

side is positive and it is necessary that $x_c > x_n > x_i$, i.e. the informal sector has the lowest productivity in case of stagnant output with full absorption of the dispossessed in the informal sector. Similarly, with no excess demand Δ for natural resource, i.e. N = 0 and h = 1, we would have a similar ordering, $k_c > k_n > k_i$ as a necessary condition. Since this ordering of productivities of sectors is derived by postulating a stationary state either in output (X = 0) or demand supply balance in natural resource (N = 0) at h = 1, no such ordering is possible in general. For instance, in the above arithmetical example, if x_c = 3, x_n = 2, ΔL_n = 10, ΔL_c = 4, the output gained (3 × 4), i.e. 12 falls short of output lost (2 × 10) = 20 by 8. It would still be a case of zero growth with constant X provided that some or all of the dispossessed (10 – 4) = 6 find employment in the informal sector to compensate exactly that shortfall of 8, i.e. at h=1, productivity of that sector would be x_i = (4/3); if h = (2/3), x_i = 2; if h =(1/3), x_i = 4. It is possible to construct examples in which the productivity of the informal sector is higher than that of the corporate sector, e.g. for h_i < (4/9) in this particular example with stationary output.

7

Climate Change of Another Kind

Like vegetation that changes with climatic conditions, economic policies too change with the climate. But it is a different kind of climate; the climate of economic opinion. Both are consequences of industrialism, particularly the idea of rapid industrialization as an unavoidable component of economic development. Nevertheless there is an important difference. Changes in the climate of economic policy impact more directly and immediately on our everyday life compared to changes in the global physical climate. And yet, while physical climate change receives a good deal of attention and research, economic climate change is seldom noticed and rarely commented upon. This is hardly surprising. Since the change in the climate of economic opinion is usually brought about by governments, a sufficiently pliable media beholden to them, and their equally pliable economic experts who become influential by virtue of proximity to political power and influence, changes in the climate of policy are orchestrated and presented to the public as necessary reforms, indeed compulsions of the day. The changes can then go largely unopposed even unnoticed under the syndrome of TINA (There Is No Alternative).

Things are more apparent when political power is heavily concentrated. Fascism required state power to be under the control of big business. Official communism wanted it under 'the dictatorship of the proletariat" (read the Communist Party). Between these extremes lies the spectrum of liberal democracies which come in a bewildering variety, from social democracy to the stance of a minimalist state and "free market".

Nevertheless they all remain capitalist democracies, rejecting neither capitalism nor political democracy but changing the definition according to the requirements of maintaining power. One common underlying presumption that gives them widespread political legitimacy is the assumed neutrality of the state to balance conflicting interests of contending classes and groups under capitalism. Even Hitler pursued populist measures for full employment until his grip on power was secure. In less extreme cases, the game of liberal democracy is played with the state as the referee which lets the fortune of conflicting class interests fluctuate within limits manageable by capitalist institutions of law, property, the bureaucracy and so forth. Like a pendulum, the function of these institutions is to let class fortunes swing, but the swing will be calibrated to avoid dangerous extremes. Thus the logic of the market that depends on 'one dollar one vote' is combined with political democracy of 'one adult one vote' even in countries that have a vast majority of very poor and a few awfully rich. The two coexist in a market democracy because extremes are institutionally forbidden spaces.

The theory of demand management in capitalist democracies was developed on this assumption of relative neutrality of the state. It is associated with the name of the British economist John Maynard Keynes, although it was formulated independently around the same time by the Polish economist Michael Kalecki. The theory in a sufficiently vulgarized form became conventional wisdom for state craft ("We are all Keynesians now" remarked former US President Richard Nixon) and reappears in its present guise under the name of 'stimulus package'. The theory says that a high level of economic activity, output and employment, can be maintained by the government by keeping aggregate demand at a sufficiently high level, whenever necessary through government spending financed by budget deficit or borrowing. The political implication of the theory is remarkable for capitalism. High output and employment would benefit both the classes-employers and employees. High profit would result from high capacity utilization and a larger volume of sales and, workers can expect a larger wage bill and easy availability of jobs at high employment. It looks like a recipe for cooperative rather than conflictive capitalism, the ideal setting for class harmony in a liberal democracy.

However, the two economists who had formulated independently the same theory of demand management differed radically, not about its logic but about the future political prospect of their theory. Keynes, with all his advantages of Cambridge and class, had come to save capitalism not to bury it. Kalecki, a Polish Jew and a refugee escaping from the lengthening shadow of Nazi Germany over Europe was acutely aware of the monstrosities capitalism was capable of producing in the service of capital—Imperialism, Fascism and Nazism. With little illusion about capitalism, Kalecki foresaw the political fragility of the assumption of a neutral state pursuing even-handed economic policies to nurture class cooperation. As early as in 1943, he claimed that the theory of demand management would falter, not on its logic but on its politics.[1]

Economic theory never rules by logic but by convenience of acceptability to the powers that be. Even before the theory of demand management had gained academic respectability, demand management policies were practiced as populist measures, starting with a massive motor way ('autobahn') construction programme in Nazi Germany as a prelude to setting up its war machinery. In comparison, Roosevelt's much publicized New Deal in the USA remained a feeble attempt (deficit hardly exceeded 5 per cent of GDP between 1934-38 returning to fiscal retrenchment by 1938); other capitalist democracies were even slower to learn. The opposition to government spending financed by deficit faded under the threat of war, and war time Keynesianism maintained full employment, but only at an enormous cost of shifting resources from civilian to military production. Demand management through war expenditure may be more dangerous than 'digging holes in the ground to fill them up' for creating demand but remains an abiding attraction due to the interests of the 'military industrial complex'.

Nevertheless, in the absence of controlled experiments of physical sciences, the experience of war economies came closest to confirming the validity of the proposition that demand management by the government can sustain full employment. If actual war was needed to establish the theory, the cold war years saw Keynesian theory gradually gaining wider acceptance in official circles. As usual, politics rather than economics was the more compelling reason. The cold war meant a competition between the two systems of market capitalism and centrally controlled Soviet socialism. Despite its many weaknesses, the latter had warded off successfully the great depression of the 1930s and, maintained full employment throughout. Its attraction was strong enough for working people in capitalist democracies for the state to look for remedial actions. And, this competition between the two systems about the welfare of their ordinary citizens contributed to the wide political acceptance of the welfare state with Keynesian demand management as its rationale.

For some quarter century after the second world war (until about the first oil price shock of 1973), long years of capitalist prosperity followed. It was a period of almost uninterrupted high employment, and growth accompanied by unprecedented rising living standard of working people followed. Scandinavian social democracies had already set the standard. As the Swedish economist Ohlin had claimed, the objective of social democracies was socialisation of consumption, not of production. This is wage-led growth, with wage defined in a broader sense to include social wage of health, education, old age insurance, etc. Nevertheless, maintaining high employment and social consumption required state intervention in production on a larger scale with budget deficit and nationalization of several industries, especially public utilities like basic health and education services. For ordinary citizens this was the golden age of capitalism; but not so for the captains of industry. Their authority over the economy was gradually eroding, as workers' 'indiscipline' in the form of higher wage claims was rising in a tight labour market with the fear of job-loss losing potency.

It was transformative politics in a limited way because it reduced drastically the role of capitalists due to the rising power of trade unions and the ability of the state to maintain continuous full employment relatively independently of the capitalist class. The carefully calibrated sham politics of electoral democracy was giving way to the real politics of decisive shift in class power.

The attack on a proactive state pursuing demand management for maintaining full employment had to come from the capitalists. It started and still continues in the name of 'sound finance'. "The social function of the doctrine of sound finance", Kalecki wrote as early as in 1943, "is to make the level of employment dependent on the 'state of confidence'".[2] The climate for economic policy had to change from wage-led to private profit-led growth which means, instead of assigning independent economic power to a relatively neutral state, the focus of policy must shift to strengthening the state of confidence of private capital for investment.

Academic economists always at the service of the powerful and, never too unwilling to make a few easy bucks through consultancy, prestigious professorships and even Nobel prizes given out by the Bank of Sweden followed enthusiastically. They argued that it is irresponsible fiscal behaviour to take recourse to budget deficit even in times of recession. Modern high theory powered by a lot of algebra about how the capitalist society behaves like an optimizing individual over time with formidable foresight stretched the false analogy between the individual and the society; financial markets were seen as the most efficient information processing institutions in which nobody had the power to manipulate information. Best of all possible worlds, governments are actually an unnecessary appendage. Government debt is burden on the future generations who have to pay back just like the individual cannot escape his debt obligations. Keynesian theory which emphasized the fact that providing productive employment to the unemployed in situations of excess productive capacity would expand the current production of the society to finance at least part of the deficit without inflation or, that the state can continue to service its debt through issuing new bonds and refinancing partly its outstanding debt through issuing bonds has no place in a theory that is based on an analogy between a capitalist society and a rational individual.

The notion of distributive justice practised in the name of democratic politics too changes when improving the investment climate for private capital becomes the focus of policy. Normally, aggregate demand increases through redistribution in favour of the poor because they consume more out of their income than the rich. Nevertheless, redistribution in favour of the poor, measures to expand social consumption and subsidies for the poor financed by progressive tax rates on income and wealth are opposed on the ground that they would be detrimental to creating the right climate for private investment. A typical justification offered is the alleged inefficiency of the state in delivering services to the poor. It is conveniently overlooked that replacing the state by the market mechanism loaded in favour of the rich prices out the poor from getting these services and creates space for private profit. The failure of the state to deliver services is not faced as a political problem; instead it is pretended to have an economic solution through the 'magic of the marketplace'.

Abandoning redistribution in favour of the poor, exactly the opposite route is taken in the name of demand management. Holding the traditional theory of demand management hostage to the interest of the capitalist class, it suggests that the rich should have even more though the generosity of the fiscal and monetary policies of the state so that they have stronger incentives to invest. This meant cutting taxes for the high income brackets, reducing wealth and corporate tax and, whenever possible generating artificially asset market and real estate booms.[3] In a favourable investment climate, the rich would invest their excess funds in financial assets to make more capital gains and keep the asset market boom going. As the rich become wealthier, they borrow more against their increasing wealth, and spend more to increase aggregate demand. The aggressive assault of this private profit led growth hopes to compensate for the reduction in aggregate demand from redistribution against the poorer classes (who have higher consumption propensity) by higher private investment from the rich who are made richer through state policy to improve the climate for investment.

Globalization adds new dimensions by increasing the relative importance of the external in relation to the domestic market. Opening up economies means that domestic demand management would be less effective, especially in those economies which are highly import dependent because a significant part of the demand generated would leak out in the form of import demand. This places economies with lower international competitiveness at a double disadvantage. On the one hand they are less able to manage effectively the level of demand at home; on the other, they are able to sustain openness in trade by accumulating deficit as growing foreign debt. This provides greater scope for international capital flows to make the exchange rate and stock markets more vulnerable to capital flights. Unrestricted economic openness for an internationally less competitive country becomes a recipe of growing indebtedness and shrinking domestic demand. So the policy prescription follows: countries should enhance their international competitiveness with the objective of achieving export led growth.

Paradoxically, it is a policy supposed to be relevant in a globalizing setting and yet, it is fallacious precisely in that setting. Not all counties can achieve export surplus at the same time, for every gainer from such strategy there must be losers who continue to accumulate sovereign debt. However, this expands the market not for goods and services, but for global finance. At the same time, obsession with international competitiveness requires giving large corporations a free hand as they are best placed to take advantage of the international market through their production and distribution network. Competitiveness in the international market usually has two aspects—having a technological edge or niche and being cost competitive. Cost competitiveness, measured by unit cost, requires higher labour productivity and lower wages. Higher labour productivity without a corresponding increase in wage has the potential of increasing the profit margin per unit of sale without necessarily enhancing price competitiveness. Although the link between wage and productivity increase (or an incomes policy) was institutionalized as a further aspect of cooperative capitalism in some European countries (e.g. in 'social partnership' in Austria, 'Social market economy' in Germany) they face increasing strain like outsourcing under the pressure of maintaining international competitiveness. While foot-loose multinational corporations restrain wags by out-sourcing or shifting locations to lower wage, lower tax countries, they increase labour productivity through shedding labour by mechanization and robotics. Neither employment nor wage grows adequately even in countries that succeed in being export surplus, while countries are compelled to join a 'race to the bottom' in terms of concession in tax policies and labour laws to nurture a more favourable climate for corporate investments.

Making sure that capitalists remain in command in democracies is a game as old as universal suffrage which found ways of excluding, blacks, women and immigrants in a variety of democracies in a variety of ways. The game is played in different circumstances, but the outcome is ensured that capitalist democracies remain capitalist first and democracy only in the second place. However, a mutation in the evolution of global capitalism has appeared paradoxically also through globalization. Because globalization has increasingly been less about free trade involving free movement of goods and services and more about free movement of financial capital. From the mid-1970s the deregulation of capital markets of major industrialized nations (OECD)—a process roughly completed by the early 1980s—unleashed massive private funds moving across national boundaries. The total foreign exchange required for trade and foreign investment accounts for hardly 4 per cent of the massive daily volume of turnover in the foreign exchange market, the rest goes in various paper assets. As globalization became more a matter of global free movement of finance than of free trade in goods and services, the centre of gravity of power began to shift. Acquiring a commanding position in the real economy lies increasingly through finance. This has changed the investment climate in at least two ways. Since a currency or stock market can be set on a downward spiral with devastating consequences for the investment climate of a country, finance capital wields power as never before. Manufacturing industries have a subservient position in this scheme because, achieving export or industrial competitiveness operates on a considerably longer time scale compared to the ability of finance to change the exchange rate or the international payments situation through short term capital flows. Its immediate victim is demand management by any individual country in isolation as capital can fly out in protest against expansionist policies to destroy almost overnight the investment climate of that country. However, against the global background of 'race to the bottom' to attract capital flows, whether policies of a national government are sufficiently hospitable to finance capital is decided by a few leading financial institutions. In developing countries it used to be the World Bank and the IMF; in developed capitalist countries private credit rating agencies rated the securities and credits of corporations. As the reach of finance became increasingly global, those private credit rating agencies became the game changers. Today it is a private credit agency like Standard and Poors or Moody which through its rating of the investment climate and sovereign risk of a country rates in effect the quality of its government, its democracy.

Capitalist democracies have come the full circle through the dominance of private finance. Management of the investment climate is increasingly done through the virtual rather than the real economy, e.g. creating artificial financial asset and housing market bubble. At the same time, in the real economy inequality increases through fiscal and monetary concessions to the rich, withdrawal of welfare measures from the poor, and slow growth of employment and wages as a consequence of dangerous obsession with international competitiveness. The interest of the real and the virtual economy is reconciled through artificial bubbles, as the negative impact of growing inequality on aggregate demand in the real economy is alleviated by the asset price boom in the virtual economy. It continues for a while driven by a mechanism of positive feedback between rising asset price creating even higher demand for assets, a self sustaining process of mutual reinforcement so long as it lasts. And yet, when the bubble of rising asset prices bursts, it throws up an old question, the question of how to reconcile a growing tension between Industry and Finance. After Britain returned hurriedly to the Gold Standard in 1925, Winston Churchill observed, "…the Governor (of the Bank of England) shows himself perfectly happy in the spectacle of Britain possessing the finest credit rating in the world simultaneously with a million and a quarter unemployed…. I would rather see Finance less proud and Industry more content".[4] As a sequel to this, Josef Steindl, one of Kalecki's most distinguished colleagues reminds us: "Kalecki used to interpret the events in Britain around 1931–32 in terms of a shift of power from the City (Finance) to Industry. The interest of the City was overruled by abandoning the Gold Standard…With this tarnishing of the international image of the City, the centre of gravity of economic policy shifted to the home front in favour of domestic industries. This provided the necessary socio-political base for the acceptance of Keynesian policies".[5]

To paraphrase Marx, history repeats itself, the first time as a tragedy, the second time, if not as a farce, then as a deeper tragedy. The tragedy is the engulfing depression with rising unemployment and erosion of living conditions of ordinary citizens in capitalist democracies. With massive bail-out to financial institutions in various forms, first the US government and now (2012) Germany tries to save Finance in the Euro-zone from a crisis, but without corresponding measures to save Industry and employment in the real economy. So long as the supremacy of Finance remains the over-riding objective of economic policy, intelligent demand management policies along Keynesian lines would have no place in the political scheme. And yet, in the final analysis Finance produces intangible 'fictitious commodities' in the form of claims on real commodities among various economic agents. The real economy that produces tangible goods and services is the foundational base on which elaborate financial structures are built. Elevating Finance to a commanding height by neglecting the underlying base of the real economy opens up new fault lines in capitalist democracies. Unless a course correction takes place soon a more devastating earthquake would engulf the system in a deeper tragedy.

References and Notes

1. M. Kalecki, 1971. 'Political Aspects of Full Employment (original 1943)' in his *Select Essays in the Dynamics of the Capitalist Economy*, Cambridge University Press, Cambridge.
2. Ibid., p. 139.
3. Development and Change, 2011. Forum 2010/2011 edited by A. Saith. For a convenient recent summary with analysis see articles on the debate on 'Inequality, Imbalance, Instability' Vol. 42, No. 1, January, pp. 70–261.
4. Minutes of February 22, 1925.
5. A. Bhaduri and J. Steindl, 'The Rise of Monetarism as a Social Doctrine' in *Post Keynesian Economic Theory* edited by P. Arestis and T. Skouras, Wheatsheaf/Harvester, Sussex, 1985, pp. 57–58.

8

What Remains of the Theory of Demand Management in a Globalizing World?

Even as societies change, powerful social theories survive, not as a coherent body of reasoning but in a 'vulgar' form. The vulgar version is not mere simplification but more like a dogma without foundation in reasoning. And, when this vulgar version enters political discourse it undergoes yet another mutation. It can be used to justify very opposite policies than was originally intended.

The vulgar version of Keynesian demand management theory to which almost all politicians irrespective of their political colour turn in times of recession is known currently as the 'stimulation doctrine', i.e. stimulating the economy with liquidity from the government and the central bank to save primarily financial institutions. However, it is hoped this will also revive aggregate demand sufficiently to save not only banks but also the real economy suffering from unemployment and excess capacity. This Keynesian policy is pursued however without any appreciation of the fundamental foundations of the theory even in the academia. Indeed most mainstream academic economists, even those who believe themselves to be 'Keynesians' continue to theorize in their technical works in a neo-classical mode. It is characterized by assumptions like representative maximizing agent(s), long run equilibrium positions from which the problem of effective demand has been banished as a 'short term' problem and, perfect flexibility of prices and wages with substitution between capital and labour induced by relative prices to reflect relative scarcity the central mechanism for equilibrating the economy at full employment. Only deviations allowed in this neo-classical scheme are short-term failure of the price mechanism due to incomplete information.

And yet, the core of the theories of Kalecki and Keynes (despite some differences especially in dealing with money and income distribution) are derived from an altogether different set of propositions. The essential propositions are:

The analogy between the individual (household) and the economy does not hold due to the circular flow between expenditure and income in the macro-economy where in a double entry national accounting format my expenditure becomes your income. As a result, expenditure injected in the circular flow (as autonomous investment) can generate matching amount of saving by raising income through the multiplier. In this framework higher saving is the consequence of higher investment, and the maximizing principle of the individual agent deciding between present and future consumption(saving) is, to say the least, is an inessential detail.

In situations of recession the generation of additional income in response to higher expenditure is mostly brought about through increase in production, as quantities rather than prices respond more vigorously at higher speed even in the short run to higher demand caused by higher autonomous expenditure.

This inverts both Marshallian and Walrasian presumption that prices rather than quantities adjust in the short run.

In this scheme prices respond to money wages and the level of output responds to the level of demand (expenditure) to permit an approximate separation between determination of prices and quantities. More importantly, the real wage rate becomes an endogenous outcome of the interaction between the price level and the money wage rate which makes the real wage rate an unsuitable policy instrument. Since wage bargain is in money terms only the money wage rate can be changed with indeterminate effect on the extent of change in the price level and the real wage rate.

The theory of demand management was set deliberately in the context of a closed economy without foreign trade to avoid unnecessary debates and detours about the unfortunate experiences of 'beggar-thy-neighbour' policies of competitive devaluation of inter-war years as they amounted to efforts at exporting unemployment. The focus instead was on national policies directed towards domestic markets.[1] The context of the theory has changed drastically with globalization.

Old trade rivalries has not disappeared in this new setting but has reappeared in different guises as national economies lost direct control to varying degrees over their exchange rates in a flexible exchange rate regime dominated by private traders. In single currency areas (e.g. European Union) no space is left for competitive devaluation, and trade rivalry takes the form of competitive unit cost reduction through national policies for real wage restraint and enhancing labour productivity, the former reducing the size of the domestic market and, the latter producing more output at the cost of employment. As a result the profit margin and share tend to increase weakening consumption demand at home, and the net effect is for a desperate zero sum game pushing simultaneously all countries of the single currency area towards export-led growth inside or outside the area to make a return to the 'beggar-thy-neighbour' policies in a different guise. Losers in this game accumulate debt, government debt, commercial debts for individual firms and households which is taken over ultimately as national debt while facing austerity measures in a situation of worsening employment situation at home through a shrinking domestic market on account of falling wage share, austerity measures and import surplus. The success of the winners on the other hand manifests in accumulating assets, mostly as government guaranteed liabilities of debtor member countries in the single currency area.

Globally the situation is similar in many ways. The perspective of shifting emphasis from the foreign to the domestic market proposed originally in the theories of demand management is reversed everywhere. Trade rivalry takes the form of targeting competitive unit cost reduction (including lower inflation to improve real exchange rate) at the cost of employment generation at home. A particular national currency (US dollar instead of the British sterling) still plays to a large extent the role of international 'money' as a medium of exchange (e.g. in oil and major international insurance contracts) as well as a store of value. This bestows on the concerned debtor country issuing the 'international money' the privilege to finance its trade deficit and other payments like investments (in real estates, natural resource acquisition etc) by letting debt instruments to accumulate abroad denominated in its own currency. Export surplus countries hold voluntarily these debts as international money. It remains a matter of speculation, how long this international exchange of paper liability for real goods and services would remain a viable arrangement. However, academic discussions usually miss the point. Unlike in the case of Britain's attempt to resurrect (1926) and subsequently abandon in humiliation the Gold Standard (1931) in face of an onslaught of downloading of sterling for gold by the rival economic powers, France and the United States, the current situation is somewhat different. Apart from providing important export outlet, the defence dependence of the important trade surplus countries (like Japan, Germany, Saudi Arabia) on the US as the military super power virtually ruled out such aggressive financial diplomacy. And yet, the emergence of China as a massive trade surplus country with independent military power has introduced an unknown variable in the system. While China too depends substantially on the US export market, the possible use of massive dollar surplus to challenge the hegemony of the dollar remains an open question.

Globalization has brought about a shift in emphasis with the external market gaining steadily in relative importance of over the internal market. This means not only greater openness to trade in goods and services, and in direct foreign investment, but openness to trade in financial assets. Countries are more tightly linked through a denser network of trade in goods and services driven to a significant extent by multinational firms. It is also the same engine which drive foreign investment in the creation of new physical assets. However, far more important has been the globalization of finance by multinational banks and other financial institutions through creating ever increasing volume of debt contracts as derivative claims and insurances on the same set of 'underlying' physical assets for trade in foreign exchange denominated assets. Indeed, because of its sheer quantitative importance, this demarcates a new period of financial globalization in which trade in financial assets completely overwhelms in quantitative significance all other trade in goods, services and foreign direct investments in physical assets.[2] They are assets traded as titles and entitlements in secondary (spot and futures) market, arising from different layers of claims of indirect or partial ownership, insurances and guarantees derived from existing 'underlying' assets. These derived claims can be created and multiplied as debt contracts almost at will by the specialized institutions of big finance with high financial standing. The centre of gravity in international finance shifts gradually as 'shadow banking' trading heavily in private debt instruments develops in a thinly supervised financial sector which escapes on the one hand supervision of the monetary authority but foregoes on the other any formal guarantee provided by the 'lender of last resort'. It creates instead its own extensive network of mutual private debt contracts, guarantees and insurances. In 'normal' times, the trust in large, private financial institutions is high and, the debt contracts circulate as privately guaranteed 'credit money'. However, somewhat like in an explosive chemical reaction they act not merely as catalysts speeding up the reaction, but produce even more catalysts to accelerate the process. In a closed self-referential system massive amounts of private debt contracts as credit money becomes available on demand for fueling demand for financial assets which are merely other forms of private debt contracts differently packaged for financial investments. This system works well and is pre-disposed towards asset price inflation to keep expectations of capital gains alive.

The asset portfolio of a country undergoes changes in composition due to expectations of changes in exchange rate, monetary (e.g. interest rate) and fiscal policy (e.g. corporate tax rate) of the national governments affecting expectations of capital gains and losses on asset prices. Since assets are denominated in different currencies and held by nationals of different countries, portfolio changes entail cross border and cross currency transactions with the result that expectations of capital gains and losses impact significantly the composition of existing portfolio of assets. This is a two way process: while national economic policies affect expectations of capital gains and losses, they in turn affect national exchange rate policies through the channel of international capital flows.

The fear of capital outflow that may be induced by the fiscal policy of the government sets a serious constraint on traditional demand management policies. Unless the sentiments of the financial market is respected sufficiently to keep 'high finance' happy, capital flight becomes a threat to a stable economic environment. Kalecki had foreseen this possibility (1943) while discussing the political viability of full employment policies over time and its impact on the 'investment climate' of a country. He had argued that the compulsion of maintaining the authority structure in a capitalist democracy requires the capitalists to retain the initiative of managing the economy by disciplining the workers and, having a commanding position in relation to the state. Continuous high employment attained through budget deficit and public spending allows the initiative of policy making to pass from the captains of industry to the hands of the government. It also weakens the threat of job-loss to workers. The authority structure of a capitalist democracy flourishes instead, if demand management is made to rely on creating a favourable climate for private investment Therefore proactive budgetary policies in favour of full employment are resisted and, denying the basic tenet of demand management, it falls back on the false analogy between the individual and the society in the name of 'sound finance' and insistence on the virtues of balanced budget. Given his historical context, Kalecki emphasized the climate for long-term industrial investment. In contemporary circumstances it would be more relevant to talk of the climate for financial investment which is highly mobile and typically short term. This makes the constraint of capital flight even more acute as national economic policies has even less manoeuverability, and have to keep the financial sector happy almost on a day-to-day basis.

In the context of an open economy the circular flow between total expenditure and income in national accounts implies the identity that an excess of private, corporate or government expenditure (investment) over its income (saving) has to be balanced by a corresponding current account deficit if other sectors maintain in co-expenditure balance. For developing an argument in favour of the private investment climate, the excess of government expenditure over its revenue is singled out without any convincing economic reason as the main causal factor in this identity for causing current account deficit on the assumption that other sectors are in balance.[3] Since consistent current account deficit can set off a downward spiral of expectations of capital losses on financial assets leading to further capital flight far beyond the initial current account or government budget deficit, it threatens a national currency with the spectre of uncontrollable depreciation.

In the changed circumstances of globalized finance with massive capital flows, the theory of demand management appears to lose its policy relevance. But appearance is not always reality! Demand management policies returned disguised in an unrecognizable vulgar form, compatible with the economic 'austerity measures' in the name of 'sound finance' which restricts government spending and, helps to establish the authority structure of finance dominated capitalism. An acid test of the validity of a social theory, Joan Robinson had perceptively observed, can be judged only when it is separated from its ideological rhetoric. A theory passes this test, when a person changes political side (say) from the Left to the Right, but continues to make use of the same theory.[4] Recent experiences would suggest that the theory of demand management passes this test.

Financial globalization and the possibility of interest induced movements of international capital flows increased the importance of monetary policy. With that came a change in the direction of policy of separating monetary from fiscal policy institutionally through the independence of the central bank and targeting inflation rather than employment. Multinational firms with subsidiaries in many countries weakened steadily the ability of governments to collect taxes, as foot loose corporations showed their profit in the countries with lower tax rates through 'creative transfer pricing', sub-contracting and threatening to move to more hospitable climates for investment. A competitive reduction in corporate tax rates (followed by later attempts at tax harmonization) under a regime of relatively mobile capital in relation to less mobile labour steadily increased the ratio of tax on wages and salaries to corporate profit. The uneven sharing of tax burden fuelled tax payers' dissatisfaction with high taxes which got directed towards inefficiency of public spending by the welfare state with considerable help from corporate controlled media. In this background, rolling back the state sector through greater tax cut for the rich became a politically more acceptable strategy even in former social democracies.

However, such redistribution policies in favour of the rich are flawed from the point of view of sustaining aggregate demand in so far as the rich have a higher propensity to save. Rising asset prices provided a way of reconciling Keynesian demand management with fiscal policy induced inequality. Enhancing the emerging authority structure of financial rather than industrial capital the market for financial assets (including housing and real estate as important variables 'underlying' many assets) the benefit of tax cut was extended further to the rich who own a disproportionately greater proportion of such assets. Cheap money and deregulation helped in sustaining high prices for financial assets as private debt contracts. Buoyant expectations about rising asset price raised simultaneously borrowers' credit worthiness and improved lenders' balance sheets. Indeed with expectations of continuing capital gains, borrowers could service their growing debt from capital gains while lenders could increase both the volume and margin of lending. A debt driven consumption boom seemed to resolve the nagging problem of effective demand while consolidating the supreme position of authority of the financial sector in the economy. The old Keynesian model of cooperative capitalism in which the state helped to sustain sufficient level of demand to maintain both high employment for workers and high profit for industrial capitalists from a high volume of sales gave way to the model of 'Great Moderation' which celebrated the supremacy of the financial sector. Capital inflow attracted by the lure of high capital gains added to the celebration by hiding problems of chronic trade deficit due to high private consumption by borrowing.

The financial sector can present a show of prosperity increasingly delinked from the working of the real economy so long as prices of financial assets continue to rise. And, sustaining expectations about rising asset prices through increased borrowing for consumption becomes the central mechanism on which this model hinges. Unlike public investment through deficit financing by the state which is meant to lift the economy out of a depressed state of private expectations about profits, this model of 'great moderation' is subject to the fragility of high expectations about private profit from asset price rise. So long as the real economy expands with asset price rise, private debt might be expected to rise faster than public debt sustained by various new debt instruments. They may even be multiplied by various derived private debt contracts of mutual guarantees from the shadow banking sector without either central supervision or a lender of last resort. In this process, the distinction between 'money' guaranteed by the monetary authority and various private credit contracts and insured privately issued and insured by the financial sector becomes increasingly blurred. They are created endogenously by the profit seeking private financial sector to exploit as well as create new demand for financial assets. This expansion of private credit without restraint fuels further asset price rise. It raises the lure of exceptional returns especially from esoteric assets while a self-referential private credit rating system as a creature of the financial system itself gains importance in underplaying risks in order to keep the show going. And, private credit rating agencies become the guardian legitimizing the system, rating not only private credit but also sovereign risk meant to rate fiscal policies of a government in terms of its impact on financial markets.

As this process continues the financial system tends to delink itself increasingly from the performance of the real economy in terms of employment and output. The turning point may come in a manner similar to the Ponzi game, but on a macroeconomic scale. It is reached when even higher returns have to be promised on financial investment to keep asset prices rising which also changes the composition continuously from real to financial investment. However, financial investment encouraging further financial investment for acquisition of claims (and derived counter claims) on existing assets does not help the real economy in raising demand for goods and services but raises the price of assets. In a more extreme case the real economy may stagnate or even decline while the prices of financial assets and the stock market continue to rise delinked for a while from the state of the real economy. This is the prelude to a financial crisis as the divergence grows between the real and the financial sector of the economy. The probability of default in the real sector increases with stagnant income but rising debt and high asset price. At this point of the Ponzi game, even a small event of default can suddenly push the fragile financial sector to a crisis. Defaulted loan has to be covered by liquidity guaranteed by the central monetary authority as lender of last resort (money) and private unguaranteed credit is no substitute, but the elaborate network of expanded private credit contracts is incapable of providing it. Every player in the financial sector now wishes to have their loan secured with adequate liquidity, but liquidity is in short supply as everyone had expanded credit contracts through private guarantees. A financial catastrophe due to sudden freeze of credit looms large.

The irony of the situation is that, such a collapse of the private financial system can be avoided only by injecting liquidity into the banks by the central monetary authority and government. Largely deregulated private banking and its private system of credit creation has to be rescued by a government which otherwise has been restraining its own budget by reducing social benefits to the poor. This is the prescription offered by both captains of industry and finance for improving climate for private investment, but they now need the government to deficit finance their rescue package!

However, even this might not be the final irony and the end game of resorting to Keynesian style demand management, while being in constant denial about its efficacy. Flooding banks and the financial sector with injected liquidity is of limited use when the private investment climate remains depressed in the aftermath of a financial crisis. In a stagnating economy there are not many who are willing to undertake long-term investment in real assets. The financial sector is salvaged with liquidity but the real economy continues to stagnate with high unemployment and excess capacity. In an economy in the grip of a long recession, under the compulsions of democracy the ultimate irony may turn out to be the old remedy of massive public investment with deficit financing to restore confidence in the climate for private investment!

References and Notes

1. Based on recollections of two separate conversations with Josef Steindl, a colleague of Kalecki in Oxford and, with Joan Robinson, a colleague of Keynes in Cambridge.

2. According to BIS statistics, the volume of trade in the foreign exchange markets increased from a daily 60 billion in 1983 (when all the capital accounts of OECD countries had been deregulated) to 1490 billion in 1998 and, the ratio of foreign exchange transaction to world export rose from world export 12:1 to 100:1 during the same period. The central banks together had a reserve of 1550 billion in 1997 hardly sufficient to cover a single day's trade in the foreign exchange. For more details see, D. Nayyar ''Globalization, History and Development', *Cambridge Journal of Economics*, 2006, 30:139–57.
3. J. Steindl, 'The Control of the Economy', Chapter 16, pp. 216–28, *Economic Papers, 1941–88*, Macmillan, London,.
4. J. Robinson, *Economic Philosophy*, Chapter 1.

9

Effective Demand Under Financialization: An Analytical Introduction

Consider an idealized economy producing only two goods: a consumption good (like rice) for current consumption and, an investment good (like tractor) which is not consumed immediately, but is needed as means of production to help current, (e.g. seeds) production; or, to augment future production capacity (e.g. tractor). Such theoretical distinctions by categories are necessarily fuzzy in real life, e.g. one can have rice seeds which can be consumed but become investment good when reserved to augment future production; the services of a tractor as investment good becomes consumption good when used for current transport of passengers. Nevertheless, to set out the argument with clarity, it is analytically necessary to distinguish current consumption from future consumption. Moreover it points to the complexity that many goods once produced become specific in their use as consumption or investment goods and, cannot be shifted easily from one use to another (tractors cannot be converted into rice without the intermediation of trade in the market which may or not be possible, costly or time consuming). Nevertheless, in standard economics using production functions this difficulty is ignored by assuming that 'capital' is instantly malleable and can change forms, say from plough to tractors, at different capital output ratios to suit relative scarcities of factors of production reflected in their relative prices.

In the basic model, we assume an economy closed to foreign trade and, place it in the short period context. This means capital goods remain non-malleable and specific to a sector within that period and the employed workers are divided between the consumption and investment goods sector. Each worker employed in the consumption goods sector produces 10 bags of rice and, is paid a *real* wage of 6 bags of rice, leaving a surplus of (10 – 6) = 4 bags of rice per worker per year. The analytical importance of surplus is twofold. First, it will be seen to be the source of profit for the capitalist employer. However, the surplus has to be realized as profit in general purchasing power of money. This requires a market in which it can be sold and, the price at which it can be sold is fixed and is above the production cost. Again, to keep the argument at its simplest we will assume that wage is the only cost, although domestically produced raw material costs could be integrated into the argument through the method of vertically integrated production (e.g. Leontief inverted matrix technique with further extentions; see Leontief, 1947; Pasinetti, 1981). However non-reproducible or imported raw materials cannot be handled easily in this way (cf. Kalecki, 1971).

However, workers producing investment goods (like tractors) cannot live by eating tractors. Their real wage must also be in consumption goods. This points to an important distinction between product wage which can be counted in any commodity like tractor and real wage in terms of consumption goods which enter the workers' budget. This distinction appears unimportant if wages are paid in the generalized purchasing power of money wage and yet, workers would be more concerned about their real wage.

We circumvent these complications for the time being by postulating that workers in the investment sector are also paid wages in the same consumption goods. If the real wage rate is assumed to be the same six bags of rice in both the consumption and the investment goods sector, then the surplus produced by workers in the consumption sector must sustain the consumption of workers in the investment sector. We consider the simplest case and assume that workers consume the entire wage bill paid to them, and save nothing. Capitalists on the other hand who employ them are presumed to do the opposite. They save everything and consume nothing! This extreme assumption can be relaxed easily by assuming that different classes have different propensities to save (as many post Keynesians following Ricardo assume, e.g. Kaldor, 1956) or, by assuming that all households, rich and poor, have the same saving propensity in passing.

Returning to the basic model let, L_i = number of workers in the investment sector and, L_c = number of workers in the consumption sector. We set up the inter-sectoral balance equation for consumption goods (first noticed by Marx) which clears the market for consumption goods. The physical surplus consumption good per worker in the consumption sector is (10-6) L_c. Since this surplus is in excess of consumption by workers engaged directly in the production of consumption goods (6 L_c), it has to find a market outside the self-consumption by workers of that sector for being sold and converted into monetary profit. This suggests the crux of the Kalecki-Keynes theory of effective demand. Commodity production is for the market and, surplus goods in excess of consumption by those directly engaged in its production generates monetary profits through the capacity of the market to absorb the surplus which in turn is determined by investment, i.e. demand for consumption goods by those not engaged in its production. With extensive division of labour and specialized production by industries, every line of production would face this problem, e.g. workers in even a typical consumption goods industry like shoes would consume only a fraction of their own production while the rest has to find a market to be realized into monetary profits. Otherwise it will remain just physical surplus in the form of inventories (planned or unplanned) without being realized into monetary profits. In the simple model with only two industries (or sectors), that market has to be provided by the demand for consumption goods by workers in the investment sector (L_i) in the form of their wage bill $6L_i$ on the simplifying assumption that capitalists do not consume anything.

The failure to make a clear distinction between surplus in physical terms and surplus realized as monetary profit leads to a typical fallacy of 'supply side economics'. It fails to realize that producing more physical surplus does not mean more profit for the capitalists. It only means greater potential for profit in a monetary economy. In the above example the selling of the surplus to the investment sector and the realization of the entire physical surplus into profit in this specific example implies, $6L_i$ (demand for surplus wage goods) = $(10 - 6)L_c$ (supply of surplus wage goods).

In symbols this provides the consumption market clearing equation,

(1) $w\,L_i = (x - w)L_c$, w = real wage rate per worker in terms of consumption goods and, x = net output (or productivity) assumed constant per worker in the consumption goods sector.

When properly interpreted this almost trivially simple equation assumes considerable economic significance. It raises the question, whether the amount of surplus generated in a capitalist economy from the supply side, i.e. $(x - w)L_c$ determines or is determined and the level of investment expenditure wL_i. Or, the level of investment should be taken as the predetermined exogenous variable of the system? This would mean that investment expenditure is determined *independently* of the level of surplus generated in the consumption sector. Mainstream neo-classical macroeconomics claims that the available surplus determines investment. It is perhaps the most important distinction between neo-classical and Keynesian economics. It is presented in various forms, sophisticated or unsophisticated, but all boil down to various restatements of the supply side economics. Because, if all surplus produced can be sold at the given price by assumption, there cannot be a problem of insufficient size of the market due to lack of demand, and no distinction needs to be made between physical surplus as a source of profit and realized monetary profit. In other words, the consumption goods market would always be clear without ever facing any problem of insufficient demand and, firms would not have to cut down employment because they cannot sell enough.

Neo-classical economics introduces apparent sophistication in the form of saving by postulating that saving is either the result of inter-generational transfer or the outcome of rational choice of one representative individual of infinite life. Saving as an inter-temporal choice is determined by the subjective time preference and diminishing utility from consumption by that single rational individual agent. The absurdity of inter-temporal rational choice assumption for examining the macro-dynamics of modern capitalism should be obvious to anyone who does not believe that we live in the best possible world. An alternative assumption about saving would be all individuals save only in their working age and dissave to consume in their old age (as in inter-generation saving models in neo-classical theory (Samuelson, 1958; Diamond, 1965)). In the latter case, savings become transferable claim from one generation to the next through IOUs permitting trade among generations which emphasise demographic rather than class distinction. The model in theory should extend from generation to generation up to infinity. However, carried to its logical extreme it raises puzzles about inter-temporal trade over infinite time horizon which may be noted only in passing.

Both inter-generational transfer and inter-temporal optimum saving model mislead because, no matter how one sophisticates the formulation about saving they are unable to see the basic point of the theory of effective demand. It is that investment decisions are independent of saving decisions. Their fundamental flaw arise not so much from the specific theories of determination of saving they offer, but in the independent role they assign to saving by ignoring the simple fact that saving is mostly made out of income, and one needs a prior theory of income determination. Postulating that saving is determined independently and, is automatically investment leaves no room for raising the problem of demand deficiency and profit realization. Instead it has to assume that whatever surplus the consumption sector produces would be sold to the investment sector and quite naturally it leads to the next false step. The consumption sector would produce to maximize its monetary profit without any fear of lack of sufficient demand in the market. Full employment or full capacity utilization would be the outcome and the consumption goods market would be cleared at that full employment level of output and all surplus realized in monetary profits. Elaborate sophistication in formulating the saving function as the determinant rather than the determined variable hides the basic question that investment sector determines the size of the market for the consumption sector in the relation between the consumption and the investment sector shown in equation (1) Nevertheless, such misplaced sophistication serves a useful ideological purpose of presenting capitalism as the most rational of all possible systems where saving is the result of optimal decisions of rational individuals, and full employment prevails with no excess capacity or unemployment arising due to lack of adequate demand in the market.

Mathematically however, equations merely balance. They cannot distinguish between a dependent and an independent variable. That is the task of theory. When written as an equation, relation (1) shows just the demand for consumption goods in the market that absorbs the surplus produced. Sales expectations of the capitalists are satisfied if that is the amount they actually expected to sell when they undertook that level of production. Only in that case there would be no unexpected accumulation due to over-optimistic expectation resulting in insufficient demand or unexpected running down of inventories due to over-pessimistic expectations about the market size. However there is no reason why this must happen because there is no market mechanism by which the decision of the investors are coordinated with that of the savers. Two possible detours to soften this coordination failure are often suggested by a class of 'neo-Keynesian' theories which appear Keynesian only to restore neo-classical orthodoxy. The first route is to suggest prices and money wages are totally flexible so that real wages would adjust to balance the demand for the surplus with its supply. Thus the physical surplus would always be realized in money profits. Nevertheless, it is seldom recognized that even in this case the money profit that is realized may not be in line with expectations because the margin between price and money wage adjusts. The second route is to focus on the price at which loans are offered or the interest rate and claim that surplus (or saving) would always be matched by its demand (or investment), as if the job of the financiers is to clear the market for loans rather than make maximum profits.

However, there is a more fundamental difference between the neo-Keynesian and Keynesian view. The view that output rather than price adjusts to the level at which it generates enough surplus to match the higher demand for surplus created through investment proves difficult for conventionally trained economists. They are used to thinking mostly of price adjustments to any mismatch between demand and supply and, for them an increase in demand due to increased investment should lead to an increase in price and not in quantity. The idea that quantity rather than price is the central adjusting variable to higher demand was a novelty that Kalecki and Keynesian introduced to change the way we think about macroeconomic problems (Leijohnhofud, 1968). It maintains that, except in situations close to full employment or full capacity utilization, significant scope exists for quantity adjustment to meet additional demand created by higher employment. This is especially true in situations of severe recession due to extensive under-utilized capacity and unemployment, but true only to a lesser extent in more normal situations as market economies tend to be operating well below their potential output (GDP) levels. To concentrate only on the failure of the price mechanism is to miss the wood for the trees and, ignore the most obvious theoretical consequence in terms of the possibility of quantity adjustment in the presence of high unemployment and excess capacity.

Balance equation (1) may be rewritten in proportions to bring out its further implications:

(2) $(L_c/L_i) = w/(x\text{-}w)$.

In the above numerical example, the proportion of labour employed in the two sectors becomes 3/2, and violating this proportion of employment distribution between the two sectors causes demand supply imbalance in the consumption goods market. If we assume capital goods are strictly specific and non-transferable in their use at least in the short period, this can be considered as the 'proportionality problem' (of Marx). It means that the given structure of capital goods, i.e. the way they are distributed between sectors is such that market clearance is impossible due to specificity (or non-malleability in Joan Robinson's terminology) of capital goods.

Written differently in terms of increments of labour employment,

(3) $\Delta L_c = (w/x\text{-}w)\ \Delta L_i = (3/2)\ (18) = 27$.

However, suppose that the market was initially cleared. In accordance with their expectation of future profits capitalists decide to employ additional $\Delta L_i = 18$ workers in the investment sector which financiers also consider profitable to finance. With labour productivity and real wage rate assumed to remain the same at $x = 10$ and $w = 6$, the additional employment required in the consumption sector to meet the demand for consumption goods by the expanded investment sector given from (3) is 27.

This defines the equilibrium extent of expansion of the consumption sector in so far as the sales expectations of the capitalists in that sector are realized, but it need not be an equilibrium either for the investors whose decisions are treated as autonomous or, for the workers because the number of workers offered employment in the investment and consumption sector may be too few. This is why Keynesian 'equilibrium' is conditional in a special sense. Because investment is the determining variable about how much surplus can be absorbed, it depends on the expectations of the investing capitalists being satisfied. However workers may not be satisfied with such an equilibrium because their expectations in terms of the level of the real wage rate does not affect the level of investment decided independently by the capitalists. This is the meaning of the term 'investment climate' which concerns capitalists' not workers' expectations. Improving the investment climate merely means inducing capitalists to expect a better market conditions for higher profit.

Returning to the above example, the direct increase in demand for consumption goods, $w\Delta L_i = (6)(18) = 108$ bags of rice is due to the increased wage bill of 18 workers in the investment sector . And yet, according to the above calculation the output of consumption goods has to increase by a much higher amount, i.e. $x\Delta L_c = (10)\ (27) = 270$ bags. This is because 27 additional workers in the consumption sector themselves consume, $w\Delta L_c = (6)\ (27) = 162$ bags of rice, and only the surplus above their own consumption, i.e. $(x - w)\Delta L_c = (270 - 162) = 108$, matches exactly the increased demand for consumption goods by workers in the investment sector. Since surplus is only a fraction of the output (or saving propensity is less than unity in conventional terms), calculated per worker is $(x - w)/x = (10 - 6)/10 = 2/5$ in this example, output has to expand $(270/108) = 5/2 = 2.5$ times to produce the required additional surplus.

This is the basic idea of the multiplier which shows that output increases several times more than demand created directly by investment (i.e. $w\Delta L_i = 108$). Quantity adjustment through the multiplier mechanism works as a convergent process like a dwindling geometric series under simplified assumptions. The series converges with a part of each round of expenditure consumed directly by the workers in the consumption sector and the rest 'saved' as surplus until the surplus is just enough to match the initial increase in the demand for surplus from the investment sector. In the above example, out of each unit of output the share of wage (w/x) gets consumed by workers in the consumption sector producing the surplus, but the rest, $(1 - w/x)$ is the share of surplus that is saved. Expanding (3) in a convergent geometric series,

(4) $[w/(x\text{-}w)]\ \Delta L_i) = [(w/x)/1 - (w/x)]\ \Delta L_c = [(w/x) + (w/x)^2 + (w/x)^3 + \ldots\ldots]\ \Delta L_c$, it is seen that (w/x) defines consumption expenditure out of each output (income) which propagates as it becomes the income of someone else in the economy, while the rest $(1 - w/x)$ generates surplus. Thus the first term of the series on the extreme right hand side represents the wage demand from injecting an additional unit of investment expenditure because the surplus per unit $[(1 - (w/x)]$ is not spent by assumption. The fraction spent (w/x) becomes the additional income (w/x) of workers and capitalists in the consumption sector in the next round. Out of their share of this next round of income, workers receive and consume $[(w/x).(w/x)] = (w/x)^2$,while capitalists save by assumption their entire income. So workers' expenditure $(w/x)^2$ becomes the income in the next round for wage and profit recipients in the consumption sector leading to further expenditure $(w/x)^3$, and so on. This gives rise to the geometric series which converges as (w/x) is less than unity and, the convergent series is merely summed up in (3) to give the total increase in demand in the consumption sector. But the expansion of the consumption sector also increases the surplus generated in each round till it matches the additional demand created by the investment sector.

Central to the multiplier process is the view of income and expenditure as a circular flow. Demand created at each round of expenditure by some becomes the income of some others in this circular process economy; and from each round of income received a fraction is consumed but the rest is saved. Since the fraction saved is withdrawal from the expenditure stream in each round, the income expenditure balance in the economy requires the withdrawals through saving through various rounds of expansion of the multiplier as an endogenous variable, and it is balanced in equilibrium by the increase in injection of expenditure through investment as the exogenous variable. Thus the multiplier implies investment saving balance which is only another way of saying that the surplus generated in the consumption sector is realized as profit through demand created by the investment sector.

However, a mistake is often made in assuming that the multiplier mechanism only expands demand or it is a process of income expansion without necessarily a counterpart in terms of production. And, it is suggested that Kalekci-Keynes theory does not have a "supply side". An inspection of the above convergent process shows that at each round of the multiplier the expansion of demand has to be matched by an increase in supply which creates income for workers as wage and income to capitalists as profit. In a process of circular flow, expenditure creates income by expanding production and distributing it as profit and wages.

However, as we have seen surplus produced over workers' real wage becomes money profit only if sufficient demand exists This market clearing equilibrium or profit realization equation encountered earlier (1) or (2) gives rise to the equilibrium condition for saving investment equality. Equation (2) is rewritten as,

(5) $(x - w)L_c = S_c = wL_i = W_i = \Pi_c$ to show that the physical surplus S_c of consumption goods finds a market equal to the wage bill of the investment sector W_i to be realized into money profit Π_c of the consumption sector. To this inter-sector balance showing realization of surplus consumption goods as profit of that sector, we add the realized profit Π_i of the investment sector on both sides to obtain,

(6) $(W_i + \Pi_i) = I = (\Pi_c + \Pi_i) = S$, where I is the total value added or output of the investment sector. It equals total profit Π which in turn equals total savings S of the economy because, by assumption no wage and all profit is saved.

If capitalists consume some fraction $1 > c_p > 0$ of their profit, we could extend the argument corresponding by noting that consumption out of profit C_p also has to be supported from the surplus of the consumption sector. Thus the physical surplus of consumption goods S_c gets realized into profits of that sector through the market provided by both the wage bill of the investment sector W_i and, capitalists' consumption out of profits C_p to yield an extended version of (5),

(7) $W_i + C_p = W_i + (C_p\Pi) = S_c = \Pi_c$, where $C_p = c_p\Pi$

Adding Π_i on both sides and simplifying, we return to the saving investment equality again: $W_i + \Pi_i = I = (1 - c_p)\Pi = s_p\Pi = S$, since all wage is assumed to be consumed, the entire saving S is given as its fraction $(1 - c_p) = s_p$ of total profit Π. This formulation is the critical bridge linking the theory of profit realization of Kelecki (1933/1971) with the theory of effective demand by Keynes (Keynes, 1936/1964).

If we make the assumption that all classes save a uniform proportion(s) of their income then workers save and withdraw from their expenditure sW, while capitalists also withdraw $s\Pi$ from their income as saving. Consequently, the balance equation becomes,

(8) $W_i - sW + \Pi - s\Pi = S_c = \Pi_c$

As before, adding Π_i on both sides and simplifying by cancelling total profit Π on both sides, we arrive back at the investment saving equality as, $I = s(W + \Pi) = sY$ (Keynes, 1936).

These various special assumptions about savings behaviour are of secondary importance (and more could easily be added to incorporate institutional savings in modern capitalism). They should not obscure the underlying economic insight. Investment saving equality is another way of saying how, as an equilibrium condition profit is realized in a capitalist economy and capitalists' expectation about the size of the market turns out to be correct (e.g. equation 5). And, equally importantly the size of the market is determined by investment expenditure as an autonomous variable which is not determined by saving but by expectations of profits. Severing the link between investment and saving and postulating quantity (or income) adjustment as the mechanism for equilibrium was the extraordinary insight. The equality holds only as an equilibrium condition when expected sale presumed by the investors while undertaking production turns out to be correct.

Suppose the investors made a wrong guess. The equilibrium did not hold or is disturbed. For instance the investment climate might deteriorate or the market size for the product might have just been wrongly guessed. This would happen, if for instance 16 instead of 18 workers are employed in the investment sector but all other data in the above example remain the same. From equation (3), (3/2) 16 = 24 workers are sufficient to produce the surplus (24) × (10 – 6) = 96 units of surplus consumption goods (S_c) to be realised into monetary profits by the wage bill of 16 workers in the investment sector, i.e. 16 × 6 = 96 units. Thus equilibrium condition (2) restated as (5) is satisfied with 24 workers in the consumption sector. But from the above data, actually 27 workers are engaged in the consumption sector. If the redundant (27 – 24) = 3 workers in the consumption sector are not immediately sacked, over and above their wage which is entirely consumed an additional unsold surplus of (10 – 6)3 = 12 would remain as unsold inventories, i.e. surplus which cannot be realized into monetary profits due to insufficient demand. This allows us to rewrite equation (5) now as an identity(not an equation),

(9) $(x - w)L_c(10 - 6)27 = 108 = S_c$ of which, $\Pi_c = wL_i = W_i = 6 \times 16$ is the profit realized in money = Π_c + unsold surplus as inventories of consumption goods, $(10 - 6)3 = 12 = A_c$ or, (10) S_c = money profit $\Pi_c + A_c = W_i + A_c$ (potential profit as unsold inventories).

We could add like in equation (6) the realized profit of the investment sector Π_i on both sides of (10) to obtain the saving investment identity which now includes unplanned inventories or unrealized profit A_c. If the investment sector also is unable to sell its entire product, we write,

(11) $S_i = \Pi_i + A_i$, A_i = unsold inventories of the investment sector.

Adding (10) and (11) we obtain the identity for the two sector economy as,

(12) $S = (\Pi_c + A_c) + (\Pi_i + A_i) = (W_i + A_c) + (\Pi_i + A_i) = (W_i + \Pi_i) + (A_c + A_i) = I + A$, i.e., unplanned inventories or potential profits A appear as (unintended) investment in (12) in an accounting sense which is an identity and always true.

The difference between and identity and an equation arises from the fact that the identity is true by definition for all values of the variables. Thus (12) would always be satisfied for all values of S,I and A. But an equation would be satisfied only for particular value of the variables. In this particular case $A = 0$ is the value at which the identity turns into an equilibrium condition. It means that only when businessmen's expectations about sales are exactly satisfied and there is no unplanned accumulation inventories (or unexpected running down or deccumulation of inventories) we have $A = 0$.

Even though the principle of effective demand is presented above in stark outlines, it is helpful for bringing out the basis for its policy implications in a coherent manner.

1. It operates via quantity rather than price adjustment in response to a stimulus in demand leading to investment generating its own savings from higher output or quantity adjustment. The level of saving is not given because income (output) as the main determinant of saving is not given but depends on the level of aggregate demand. Consequently saving is not a constraint and does not limit investment so long as income can expand with demand.
2. From this perspective, measures to stimulate saving through higher interest rate and similar monetary policies are typically counter-productive in so far as higher interest discourage investment by raising the cost of borrowing and debt servicing burden for government and highly leveraged firms.
3. Monetary policy and 'sound finance' by lowering budget deficit are generally counter-productive for similar reasons in recessionary situations in so far as such situations usually permit significant quantity adjustment. In case deficit is

financed through selling bonds in the market which lowers it price and raises the interest rate to crowd out private investment significantly, the answer usually lies in changing the mode of financing and letting the government borrow directly from the central bank.

4. The general thrust of Keynesian policies is to let monetary policy accommodate and support rather than oppose expansionary fiscal policies in times of serious unemployment and recession. An independent central bank that is meant to defend the currency or fight inflation by restraining government expenditure is therefore counter-productive in times of recession. The extent of its independence should be conditional, linked to the potential and actual GDP and employment situation.

Finally it is wiser to rely on fiscal policy rather than monetary policy as far as possible and, direct expansion of government spending in times of recession because, unlike monetary policies the time lags and processes involved are longer and less certain. It is important to note that the size of the market for surplus consumption goods is not determined by the workers who are engaged directly in producing consumption goods. They generate a surplus over and above what they themselves consume; so 'others' in the economy like workers in the investment sector in the present example who do not directly produce consumption good have to provide the market for its realization into money profit. Thus, generation of money profits in a capitalist economy involves two distinct steps: (a) production of surplus over the level of consumption by workers engaged in directly producing it (i.e. workers in the consumption sector in our example) and, (b) the existence of a market where the surplus is to be sold (i.e. consumption by workers in the investment sector in this example).

This leads to a paradoxical aspect of a capitalist economy based on profit incentives. Producing merely more surplus by increasing labour productivity through higher efficiency or lower wage is not enough to sustain higher money profits because it produces only more potential profit. It has to find an adequate market for realization into money profits. Similarly, the more the capitalists are able to press down the real wage to raise surplus per worker at a given level of productivity, the more acutely they face the problem of realizing a higher level of profit due to the smaller size of the market. The way out is either to raise investment or raise capitalists' level of consumption. This indeed is done often in contemporary capitalism by keeping workers wages low, but raising consumption by the richer sections through measures like generous tax concessions for the rich and manufactured asset price boom to create a market for the realization of the surplus by expanding the consumption of the rich. Indeed for realization of profit, the type of expenditure is irrelevant; it may helps or hamper income or consumption equality, may be useful or useless to the society. At least in the short run military expenditure or excursion to the moon could be as effective as say protection of environment or health care.

The context of Keynes' analysis was the 'short period' which differed from the earlier formulation of Marshall in two fundamental ways. The first was his insight that the speed of quantity adjustment dominates that of price adjustment even in the short period in a market economy in situations of substantial unemployment and excess capacity. Moreover, the signal for output adjustment in response to higher demand comes not necessarily from higher prices but from quantity signals like inventory changes, registered job vacancies, etc. For economists accustomed to the idea of the market economy as responding only on price signals this still remains a relatively novel idea to grasp.

The second novelty was his theorizing about the economy facing an uncertain future. By pointing out that money held, or more generally the liquidity positions taken by economic agents depends on their view of how uncertain the future is, money became the economic link between the future and the present money and, a channel through which the future affects the present (contradicting in standard views of causality, also in econometrics, that 'cause' precedes 'effect' in time). This has the immediate consequence that a part of income can be held in money or some other financial asset as 'store of value' to be spent in some future period. Say's law fails as wedge between income and expenditure is driven by the use of money as a store of value in every short period. This has an immediate policy implication.

Trying to stimulate demand by providing banks and other financial institutions with money or making them more liquid may not be effective, particularly when uncertainty is high. And, when uncertainty is high, and everyone is inclined to hoard more money and remain more liquid (provided the stability of the value of money is not questioned); so the level of both consumption and investment expenditure gets depressed. And for the same reason, banks and financial institution might also prefer to be more liquid. In the aftermath of a financial crisis when confidence about the future is shaken and uncertainty is high, a policy of making the financial institutions more liquid to stimulate demand is likely to be particularly ineffective. It might rescue the banks, but is no guarantee that it would rescue the economy from recession.

This leads to quite a different understanding of how the real and the financial sector interact in modern capitalism characterized by the overwhelming importance of the financial sector. Not only the focus of policy making shifts from the real to the financial sector, it tends to put the real and the financial economy in a contradictory relation. When the real economy does well for some time uncertainty begins to recede in the background and, all agents including financial institutions take less liquid position lured by prospects of capital gains in a rising stock market and also, tend to lend more on easier terms because of healthy balance sheet positions. However, with even a slight rise in the unanticipated rate of default, their relatively illiquid position makes it more difficult for them to cover the default (e.g. 'margin contraction').

Paradoxically, the greater fragility of the private financial system becomes a consequence of the good health of the real economy! It suggests a 'dual instability' hypothesis: when the real economy is stable in a tranquil expanding mode, the financial economy tends to become increasingly unstable and vice versa. Moreover, the more homogeneous are optimistic expectations about the future, the more the financial economy is vulnerable to a free fall in a frictionless system of uniform optimism. It might sound paradoxical that good health in one sector means ill health for the other sector. And yet, as Kaleki had observed, it is not the theory but the subject matter of the theory, namely capitalism, that is paradoxical!

References

1. A. Bhaduri, 1986. *The Dynamics of Commodity Production*, Macmillan, London, Chapter 2.
2. P.A. Diamond, 1965. 'National Debt in a Neoclassical Growth Model', *American Economic Review*, 55(5):1126-1150.
3. J.R. Hicks, 1969. *The Crisis of Keynesian Economics*, Oxford, Clarendon.
4. N. Kaldor, 1956. 'Alternative Theories of Distribution', *Review of Economic Studies*, 23:83-100.
5. M. Kalecki, 1933/1971. 'A Model of Business Cycles' in his *Essays in the Dynamics of a Capitalist Economy*, Cambridge University Press, Cambridge.
6. Keynes, J.M. (1936/1964). *The General Theory of Employment, Interest and Money*, Macmillan, London.
7. W.W. Leontief, 1947. *The Structure of the American Economy*, University Press, Harvard.
8. L.L. Pasinetti, 1981. *Structural Change and Economic Growth*, Cambridge, Cambridge University Press.
9. H. Minsky, 1975. *John Maynard Keynes*, New York, Columbia University Press.
10. P.A. Samuelson, 1958. 'An exact consumption-loan model of interest with or without the social contrivance of money', *Journal of Political Economy*, LXVI(6):467-482.

10

Nationalism and Economic Development

It is the paradox of our time. The paradox so thoroughly permeates the air we breathe that we are usually unaware that it is polluted, polluted willfully by the media, the politicians, the historians and the opinion makers of all sorts because their own opinions are formed by breathing in the same air. Nationalism and the nation state seem as eternal facts of life , not a passing construction of history which can be questioned.

Nationalism was meant to defend homogeneity, the right of a homogeneous group of people. However the homogeneity of the group invariably turns out to be fictitious because members of the group must have different affiliations. They are attached with varying intensity, perhaps to their region, sub- region, religion, language, ethnicity and childhood memories. A normal person would simultaneously have many such affiliations in a complex society, and what relative importance (s)he attaches to them and how they might change from time to time should remains a personal matter. This has been the polite liberal solution. However this comes into conflict when the nation is mobilized for an over-riding cause like in a war situation. All members are supposed to be united for that over-riding cause. Even without war, the loyalty to the nation state, to its territorial integrity and authority of the state in matters of law etc are ensured in the notion of 'political citizenship'. The construction of the nation state is justified in so far as it defines in this respect the political duty of the citizen. Its pitfalls are many, the danger of such loyalty has repeatedly been shown by recent history of Fascism and Nazism or even more recent unfolding history of unquestioned 'fight against terror' and, of regime change. The root of fundamentalism lies in insisting that all members of a nation state must accept a single hierarchy(or lexicographic ordering with no trade off among loyalties) in which a paramount affiliation must over-ride all others. The fact that even the liberal modern democracies insist on this loyalty in the form of 'political citizenship' which requires unquestioned loyalty to the nation state irrespective of other affiliations, does not make it easier. It is no less fundamentalist than paramount loyalty to a religion or language, only it conforms to the 'modern' idea of nationalism.

Indian nationalism in the modern sense took shape around anti-colonial struggle.It was a political project from the beginning, but neither the nation nor the nation state was quite there under colonial occupation. Since anti-colonialism was the defining characteristic, those who considered other loyalties like religion (e.g Muslims) or culture (North east, Nagas), or caste oppression (Dalits) to be more important than fighting foreign rule were treated with suspicion, often as traitors.. Congress under Gandhi became a mjoritarian nationist movement which found no way of dealing with minority rights. In this case minority right means loyalty of some other kind being more or at least equally as important as anti-colonialism. Standing in contradiction to majoritarian understanding, those who emphasized religion or Dalit oppression or class division as their primary concern found no place in the mainstream of nationalism. It put together a strange collection, Jinnah as spokesperson for Muslim rights, Fezo for rights of the Nagas, Ambedkar for Dalits or Communists inspired by the Soviet example. The majoritarianism went even further by excluding those who were dedicated even more passionately to anti-colonialism without the creed of non-violence like Bhagat Singh or Bose (Indian National Army) and several others. Looking back it was marked by all the narrowness that is typical of a political party today. Although a nation was yet to be born through anti-colonial struggle, they already added to the dictum 'my nation right or wrong', the further appendage 'my way of thinking right or wrong'. Our anti-colonial nationalism was constructed on that basis.

After independence, the Congress under Nehru got involved in nation-building using economic development as a major instrument. However social developments and minority rights were handled mostly through laws without mass movements. It was believed that higher economic growth will alleviate social problems and discriminations against minorities over time, much like the belief held by many today that higher growth by itself irrespective of its content will eliminate poverty or market will dissolve the problem of regional tensions.. The parallel goes deeper. Interim legal reliefs were given for social development, while economic development was supposed to do the bull work. Discrimination by caste, gender, religion etc was declared illegal, reservation for the disadvantaged 'scheduled' castes and tribes were provided. All governments talk today of the need for higher economic growth with legal safety nets for the socially disadvantaged, the marginalized and the poor. Our majoritarian democracy, despite differences in political rhetoric has been engulfed by the idea of legal rights for minorities.

And yet, it is a bottomless pit because everyone belongs to a minority in some sense. You may be a Hindu but belong to the OBCs and feel underprivileged, at the same time hostile to other minorities like Dalits or Muslims; or a Muslim feeling thoroughly discriminated against by a predominantly Hindu majoritarian state; or a Behari worker in Maharashtra and linguistically discriminated and so forth in an endless procession of minorities defined and redefined. To counter this, Indian democracy if anything shows greater tendencies towards an imagined majoritarianism in culture discouraging dissents for various minority rights and typically ends up by suppressing everyone's right unnecessarily. This indeed is also the most fertile ground on which the democratic politics of creating 'vote banks' thrive in our time. An imagined majoritarian nationalism plus the idea of excluding all other ways of thinking, particularly if it affects electoral prospects, is not something that has suddenly appeared on the Indian political scene. Unfortunately it is our historical inheritance!

Growth rate is a mere number. It does not require a special eye to see that without concern about distribution, other aspects of social development or its environmental impact it cannot mean much. No such summary statistic can. Yet the convergence about the need for higher GDP growth is remarkable. Just as we are afraid to question the content of nationalism, we are afraid to interrogate higher growth. The most that we hear is that higher growth must be accompanied by more social security, need for examining the trade –off between growth and social spending or environment and similar apologist's views. The challenge of questioning the logic of high growth with industrialization led by corporations in a globalized setting is seldom taken up; or those who take it up go off usually in a tangent about the need to preserve environment forgetting that people are part of the environment. This is unsatisfactory. I offer instead three inter-related propositions around which we need to to rethink economic development of India.

1. Higher industrial growth in a globalised setting would inevitably lead to greater emphasis on the external rather than the domestic market, over-emphasis on international competiveness and attempts at attracting foreign capital through measures like tax breaks, keeping the stock market high at any cost, restrictive public finance etc. This places large corporations in a highly favourable position, and paves the way for relying on corporate-led growth. As a favoured alternative it has two major and disastrous consequences despite the fact that all political parties, irrespective of their pronouncements (when out of power) and ideological colours have converged on in practice. First, at least for India, openness to trade, investment and finance can provide no immediate solution to its massive unemployment and sub-human poverty. Capital intensive corporate led growth destroys more livelihoods than it

can possibly create employment in the near future. Development in a civilized democracy must treat this problem as of utmost importance. Second, its ecological cost is not only enormous, but politically unsustainable. Difficulties faced by different governments with respect to land acquisition is a reminder of both the livelihood destroying aspect and the ecological consequences of the current pattern of development as we are reminded everyday by pollution, deforestation on the one hand and growing needs of urbanization and infra-structural bottlenecks. In this respect the debate about 'growth with social welfare' versus 'higher growth at any cost' misses the point. What we need is a reorientation of the development process, rather than how much growth with how much welfare. Our development model must deal simultaneously with extensive poverty, unemployment and ecology.

2. The guidelines for this proceeding along the new direction can be broken into four steps for simplicity of exposition.

(a) A far greater emphasis on the expansion of the domestic or internal market, particularly in the segment in which the poor work and also, draw their sustenance from, rather than on the external market. Our priority lies here without obfuscating the issue by claiming that there is no alternative to industrialization, urbanization through market oriented globalization ('Tina' syndrome).

(b) We should focus on employment creation rather than growth in GDP particularly in that segment of the internal market. Output growth should be an outcome of employment growth and not the other way round. In terms of economics it basically means 'extensive growth' where the focus is on total output through employment expansion rather than expansion through higher productivity of labour and surplus generation per unit of labour. Fiscal and monetary policies and incentives should be used to promote this. Taxation should be the necessary fraction of maximum employment oriented output for financing welfare and growth. The market principle which treats labour mainly as cost to reduce the unit cost of production(i.e. cost per unit of output) by restraining wage and increasing labour productivity should be replaced through fiscal and monetary incentives for encouraging employment oriented projects on local infrastructural development and community based projects. They can be either in the public or in the private or in the joint sector encouraged by suitable fiscal incentives. In employing this strategy it needs to be kept in mind that wage or earning of ordinary labour is the most important source of demand in the internal market. This source has to be nurtured rather than suppressed for market- oriented profit.

(c) Production and demand generation in the internal market at an adequately expanding rate for the majority is not possible in India without emphasis on decentralization as an integral part of the strategy combining simultaneous growth of demand and supply. However experience has repeatedly shown that decentralization from a top heavy bureaucratized central structure is unworkable and counter-productive. The mechanism must be one where initiatives and pressures come from lower level to force the upper level. In India the structure exists in law to some extent, but this is only on paper. Financial decentralization with local projects and initiatives chosen autonomously by lowest village level elected bodies should make the beginning. Employment guarantee schemes designed from the top are largely doomed because they are bound by uniform and inflexible financial norms set by the higher administrative bodies in the Centre and the States. Instead, we have to design a modified market principle by which local branches of nationalized banks would advance loans for specific projects without approval from above and norms for financing in each case should be agreed locally between the lender and the borrower. Unless a certain variable fraction decided at the time of lending is repaid through the operation of the project the loan would not be renewed. The local population would partly bear the cost (after a grace period) on the principle of 'he who benefits should pay' through devises such as users' cost, locally imposed taxes and complementary matching support from higher authorities. The number of users of a project would also be an indicator of the acceptability and usefulness of the project. The designing of the project would vary from case to case depending on decision taken by local bodies. There is always the possibility of local bodies being dominated by a local elite and, the safeguard is not only election by secret ballot on the acceptability of each project in the presence of the potential financier (e.g bank) but the composition of the electorate which must have sufficient representation of disadvantaged castes, women and a few random disadvantaged group observers chosen from neighbouring areas. This is far from a fool proof process but it would have a greater chance of success and would need modification through experiments. However, experience suggests it has greater chance of success if it includes a component of 'social wage' giving priority to those who construct projects to enhance social consumption like schools, health centres, water management, storage facilities etc. Along with payment of personal money wage to the workers, this would be a component of wage to indirectly raise the living standard locally especially of targeted groups. Introduction of a system of common school, health, water with management represented heavily by disadvantaged groups as a condition for subsidized loan would be highly recommended also for its social impact.

(d) Finally, it must be remembered that ecological interdependence is complex and a little understood area of knowledge. This complexity cannot be handled only by documented scientific knowledge and requires depending also on long experience of local population in each case. Both types of knowledge must be given weight. When the local bodies strongly oppose a move on ecological ground, it should be reexamined by specialists on the basis of local experience. At most limited pilot experiments rather than forcing hurried decisions on local ecological systems is a wiser option. At the same time, there is no absolute value in insisting on conservation of nature at any cost. We must recognize that order to disorder and change in that sense is an inescapable natural law. The point is to decide on what change is acceptable to the local community and, under what conditions. Many of the pressing problems like land acquisition, building dams, sanitation and even language policy in schools can be handled better this way through consultation with potential local users.

3. It would be foolish to imagine that these ideas of decentralized democracy and development can be easily accommodated in the present political system in which vested interests usually operate in a diametrically opposite way. For instance, land acquisition by governments and handing it over cheap to corporations as an investment incentive for improving the investment climate is the current preferred strategy for development. However, in effect it is a mutually beneficial arrangement between the government and corporations in so far as the latter gets land cheap, uses it partly for real estates etc for enormous profit, and returns the favour to individual politicians and political parties through donation of election funds. The corruption involved is individual as well as systemic. Any political party contesting elections feels it has better chance of success with more money and land acquisition becomes the developmental option not for people but for the corrupted politicians and parties. Similar is the case of building large dams forging an alliance between contractors and the political parties. The use of unilateral state power to usher in a particular development strategy corrupts democracy itself, and politicians, bureaucracy and large corporations join a process of their own profits and advantage in the name of 'people', helped by

corporate funded media and obliging academics as beneficiaries who help in manufacturing opinion. The resistance to decentralization for this reason would be enormous from the existing system and we must not underestimate it. Our options are limited as all electoral politics of all parties soon falls in line. Still a struggle must be on, and this is where social and political movements outside political parties can play a crucial role in constantly challenging the system. It is a long and difficult journey ahead, but even a long journey starts with a small first step. At times single issue, little local movements and resistances are the path-finders in an otherwise hopelessly complex maze of parliamentary democracy.

11

On Inequality and Economic Power

Analogies can mislead, but also illuminate at times, by providing a fresh perspective to a complex problem. The analogy that comes to my mind is the law of gravitation for discussing the link between inequality and economic power. Inequality is visible, even statistically measurable in many instances, but economic power that drives it is invisible and not measurable. Like the force of gravity, power is the organizing principle of inequality, be it of income, or wealth, gender, race, religion and region. Its effects are seen in a pervasive manner in all spheres, but the ways in which economic power pulls and tilts visible economic variables remain invisibly obscure. It defies direct empirical analysis, and has to be analysed through its effects.

Forms of Domination

Like the attraction of gravity, the exercise of power also needs more than one body. In almost all cases of power, it is expressed in different forms of domination of one body by another: the dominator and the dominated, the master and the slave, the king and his subjects, the coloniser and the colonised, the employer

---

Text of the lecture delivered on the award of the Leontief Prize for Advancing the Frontiers of Economic Thought by the Global Development and Environment Institute at Tufts University, the United States.

and the employee; relations of conflict and collaboration based on mutual dependence as well as antagonism. Forms change, the content remains more or less the same.

In many instances as the domain of domination increases, the form becomes less clear. When colonial powers dominate a country, almost invariably it has collaborators in the country and there can be unintended benefits. The British created a middle class in India which largely collaborated with the ruling powers, and yet provided a window to much of modern knowledge while suppressing traditional knowledge. This view of conflict and cooperation inherent in capitalism was brought out by a prey–predator model (Richard Goodwin's use of the Lotka–Volterra model, 1967, which I was told was mentioned by the biologist JBS Haldane to Goodwin during his visit to the Indian Statistical Institute in Kolkata, in the 1950s,) of tigers (or capitalists) living on say rabbits (or wage labour). There would be an unchecked growth of rabbits unless tigers eat them, but if they eat too many, rabbits would be in short supply threatening the existence of tigers. There is mutual dependence but it would be wrong to suggest that rabbits rather than tigers are the dominant power. In too many economics textbooks, particularly in the United States (US), capitalists can hire labour and labour can hire capitalists in a "perfect capital market," forgetting that mutual dependence does not rule out power relations. Like in a complex chemical reaction we have to isolate the relation of dominance. And the general principle is to ask whether under different institutional arrangements, which of the two parties—the prey or the predator—could survive without the other. Economic power is embedded in the institutional arrangements and the ideology that legitimises it, as I will make clearer later.

Since interaction between at least two persons is involved, it is a subject that cannot be satisfactorily dealt with within the framework of "methodological individualism." And, since the question of domination cannot be handled, it is changed to a question of differences in taste and preferences of the individual in that framework (à la Gary Becker on race). Again, it resembles the issue of mutual dependence. If I have a special taste not to have non-white skinned neighbours, the non-white skinned neighbour is welcome to have the taste of not wanting to have white neighbours. As we shall argue, the crux of power relations lies in whose choice set permits what in a society and determines the relations of domination.

In mainstream economic theory, interactions among rational isolated individuals are connected to one another only through prices and quantities in the market. They optimise, driven by their self-interests. If one were a true follower of Adam Smith, one would have made room for society to have some influence through various social norms and "moral sentiments" like trust, obedience to laws, enforcement devices for contracts, etc, to ensure the viability of the market as an institution. However, with or without these social norms in the idealised market of economic theory, individuals remain powerless except through their purchasing power derived from transactions with "initial endowments." Distributive inequality enters through the backdoor of endowments as a proxy for wealth, but the role of money vanishes as a store of value because uncertainty is banished by assumption. Without money, only relative prices matter. These prices have the usual property that while they can affect how much is bought and sold in the market through exchange, they are given parameters for all individuals irrespective of whether they are affected positively or negatively by this relative price mechanism. Those who set the "rules of the game" by organising the market and setting prices remain invisible like the force of gravity. So, like Voltaire's God, an auctioneer has to be invented to do the job of setting the market clearing prices. That invented God also prevents people from trading at non-market clearing prices. It is the story of an all-powerful auctioneer and powerless passive participants in the market.

'Market Failure'

The question of how prices are set is actually left hanging in the air as a gaping hole in the theory. It has to be so because to admit it, is to admit the raging bull in the fine china shop of well-crafted theory because it wishes to dodge the question of power. For those brought up in this intellectual tradition, this has set a mild dissident research agenda for analysing "market failures," and how wrong prices get set. The more traditional view used to be of various imperfect market forms from "monopoly power" to strategic interactions arising from competition among a few rivals and, frictions like transaction costs and high "menu cost" of changing prices frequently. The theory of games is best applied when those few competitors strategise or bargain with one another but with their strategies or options predetermined.

The current wisdom on market failure has shifted attention to information as the strategic variable, where one participant has access to (or can manufacture) more information (or misinformation) than others, to enjoy the power of setting prices. This assumption is anathema to market fundamentalists for whom prices are "public" information available to all in a market. The market processes most efficiently all available information and presents them as encapsulated current market prices to all participants, without fear or favour. No individual participant can improve upon them. Being equally informed, one price for the same commodity must hold to rule out arbitrage, special information, inside trading, etc.

Question of Economic Power

However, the debate between market fundamentalists, and those who allow for the possibility of price failures under various characterizations of imperfect information (for example, moral hazard, asymmetric information, adverse selection, etc) touches tangentially, but does not really face the question of economic power. To see this, let us put the problem in a more direct way. Suppose individual X would like to take the course of action 1, not

2. However, individual Y has the power to dominate him by making him take action course 2 instead. The question of how power is exercised is usually explained by elaborating how Y manages to do it. If we leave out the obvious case of use of brute military force threatening X to fall in line, not because it is less important in reality (indeed very important in international relations), but because there is not much to discuss, we can proceed with subtler cases of information-based power. Y might dissuade X by (i) revealing more information to X than he had about the negative consequences of following his preferred action course 1 (like a doctor explaining to the patient the likely consequences of smoking, or a scientist explaining the danger of nuclear war to a politician); (ii) doing the same, but by misinforming him deliberately and dissuading him from taking his preferred course of action (especially important in our age of media, paid news and advertisements, not to speak of esoteric financial products). Both these relate to the information aspect. However, consider a third case which is far more important for understanding the role of power in the economy and society. This is the case of (iii) closing the option for X of following his preferred course of action 1. How this is done is the essence of the broader problem of characterising power.

At the abstract level we are talking, institutions are social devices put in place not just to routinise actions, but to reduce the options or strategy sets of some and to expand that of others. More than anything else, the analysis of economic power is the analysis of institutions and their reinforcing ideologies.

The most obvious case is when state power decides what is legal or illegal through the combination of institution and ideology. Institutions imposed by the state without the consent of people have fragile foundations; they require to be legitimised by an ideology. And, it is most robust and durable when the person for whom the option is being closed consents because she is not even aware of being ruled by that ideology. For example, Adam Smith propounded the ideology justifying the market as an institution which coordinated most effectively the decisions of individuals in a society with an elaborate social and technical division of labour. He provided an ideology for the existence of the market as an institution. For Marx, the very same institution of the market had the role of making wage labour free from slavery or serfdom only to compel them into a situation of creating surplus for profit. This too was an ideology about the market. The tragedy is when you recognise one as an ideology but fail to see the other in the same light. There is a danger of dogmatism in assuming that the same ideology legitimises in all circumstances in the same way the institutional closure of options. The analysis of economic power has to be more varied and complex. Economics or any social science is not so privileged as to reduce all power relations to one cause. Marx probably came closest to it by identifying the ownership of means of production as the institution and private property as its reinforcing ideology. Together they define power relations. However, this needs modifications in each concrete situation, and I would try to illustrate this with two examples, one from developed (the US) and one from developing (India) capitalism.

Growth of Finance in the US

It is history now that the liberalization of capital markets from mid 1970s gave private traders, in place of the state, unprecedented power to trade in increasing volume of foreign exchange. This was the beginning of the phenomenal growth of the financial sector, and by the 1990s one significant segment of it more or less escaped the control of the central bank. The trading operations of private agents were neither sufficiently supervised nor guaranteed by the central bank, the so-called shadow banking sector which now exceeds in quantitative importance traditional banking. Instead of regulation, the guiding ideology became self-regulation for the entire financial and particularly its shadow banking sector. Shadow banks were the institution and self-regulation was the ideology, and they reinforced each other by creating, and mutually guaranteeing among themselves through private insurance-like schemes, various debt denominated securities to be sold as financial products.

When this scheme collapsed, large players (mostly investment banks) were bailed out through infusion of public money by the government without, however, the government nationalising or even significantly raising its stake in decision-making. The ideology of self-regulation virtually without control from outside continues with minor variations to date. Many of the financial institutions are flush with liquidity injected in the rescue operation but not many avenues to lend for productive investment in a depressed economic situation. One easy avenue open to them is creating esoteric securities with high promised returns and risk which find a market among the exceptionally rich. Their wealth grows partly on that account, irrespective of the depressed economic condition in the real economy, widening economic inequality further. This example strikes me because the most inclusive political institution of majoritarian democracy has shown up that the political logic of "one adult, one vote" and the market logic of "one dollar, one vote" are not reconcilable, if economic power is increasingly concentrated in institutions of finance under the ideology of self-regulation. Indeed, this appears almost like a critical point in the trajectory of democratic evolution, as freedom of the market amounts to freedom of rich financial corporations. An insignificant minority of rich individuals dominates the overwhelming majority in a majoritarian democracy.

However, my abiding research interest is not the misdoings of high finance through its increasing power in developed countries but in a developing country like India. Of how, despite the overwhelming poverty of the majority, economic development as an ideology has been virtually equated with corporate-led economic growth. A few among the economists are shamefaced about it, and want growth to be moderated by social welfare measures of the state; others are more forthright and support promoting unrestrained growth that might trickle down to the poor someday. Both hardliners and moderates dodge the real issue. Corporate-led higher growth means providing stronger incentives to the corporations to invest which goes under the name of a "more favourable investment climate."

Displacement in India

Beyond the usual tax breaks and concessions to business (estimated as foregone revenue it is of the same order as all subsidies to the poor majority on an annual basis in India), the government has tried to offer more powerful incentives by giving land and natural resources at virtually throwaway prices to private corporations. It displaces, on a large scale, people who lived on them. This development-induced displacement of some 0.6 million people per year is almost never of really privileged citizens, but of the poor "Adivasis," the original inhabitants of the country and, of the least privileged on the caste hierarchy, the Dalits in the countryside.

According to more than one Government of India report, the Adivasis, constitute about 8 per cent of the population but account for 40 per cent to 50 per cent of the displaced. This process, better described as internal colonization rather than creative destruction, is let loose on poor people to promote the investment climate for large corporations. And yet, because of the insufficient size of the domestic and external market (India is a systematic net importer with a negative foreign trade multiplier), corporations absorb by employment only a small fraction of those displaced. But their high natural resource intensive technologies produce more output than is lost through displacement. For instance, if 10 persons each producing 2 units are displaced from the natural economy and five find employment in the corporate sector with a labour productivity of 8 units, employment and livelihood possibilities have been halved, but output has been doubled. This is the basic recipe of corporate-led jobless growth, visible not in India alone. And, properly educated people in good schools are taught to accept this as the ideology of development and not question the dangerous obsession with higher corporate efficiency for international competitiveness, which increases further unemployment.

Dangerous Mutualism

Infusing the institution of democracy with the ideology of higher growth without considering the fate of the majority involved is made politically correct. This results in a dangerous mutualism that develops between the private corporations and the government in the name of higher growth. The corporations become exceptionally rich as never before, because of natural resources transferred to them cheap. It increases their wealth at a rate that profit from production could never match.

If privatization of state assets was Russia's way of creating most overnight dollar billionaires, India's way has been the pursuit of higher corporate-led growth! (Russia stands third and India fourth according to a recent count of exceptionally high net worth individuals). In India, the large business houses return the favour through handsome donations to political parties that make contesting elections prohibitively high for ordinary citizens without the support of a political party well-endowed with donations from the rich. In the competitive game of multiparty elections, all political parties irrespective of their political colour soon fall in line. The inclusive democracy of "one adult, one vote" in a poor (wo)man's democracy is reconciled with economic power of corporations by price rationing out the poor from any possibility of direct representation.

The result is a homogeneous mass consisting of many political parties with different colours. They are different in their rhetoric when in opposition, but same in action when in power. Choice is closed through the institution of democracy and the ideology of equating higher growth with development. As the empty shell of democracy hollowed out of its content and the march from corporate-led industrialization to corporate-led democracy continues unhindered, the need for intellectual work becomes more pressing, not to glorify the institution of democracy and the ideology of higher growth, but to challenge them with alternatives.

References

Gary S. Becker (1971): *The Economics of Discrimination*, Chicago: University of Chicago Press.

R.A. Dahl (1957): 'The Concept of Power,' *Behavioural Science*, (3):201–15.

R.M. Goodwin (1967): "A Growth Cycle," *Socialism, Capitalism and Growth*, C.H. Feinstein (ed), Cambridge: Cambridge University Press.

A. Gramsci (1971): *Selections from the Prison Notebooks*, New York: International Publisher.

J. Harsanyi (1962/1971): 'The Dimension and Measurement of Social Power,' *Power in Economics*, K. Rothschild (ed), Harmondsworth, UK: Penguin Books, 77–96.

R.J.A. Little and D.B. Rubin (2002): *Statistical Analysis with Missing Data*, 2nd edition, New York: John Wiley.

M. Rehm and M. Schnetzer (2015): 'Property and Power: Lessons from Piketty and New Insights from the HFCS (Household Finance and Consumption Survey)', *European Journal of Economics and Economic Policies: Intervention*, 12(2): 204–19.